JEFF GORDON®

Fire & Flames Edition

This publication is not affiliated with Jeff Gordon®, Jeff Gordon, Inc., J.G. Motorsports, Inc., Hendrick Motorsports, General Motors Corporation, NASCAR® or any of their affiliates, subsidiaries, distributors or representatives. Any opinions expressed are solely those of the authors, and do not necessarily reflect those of Jeff Gordon®, Jeff Gordon, Inc., J.G. Motorsports, Inc., Hendrick Motorsports, General Motors Corporation or NASCAR®. Jeff Gordon® is a registered trademark of Jeff Gordon, Inc. The likeness of the No. 24 race car is a trademark of Hendrick Motorsports.

Photo Credits
Front cover (left to right): Jamie Squire/Allsport (Gordon) AP/WWP (car), AP/WWP (Gordon)
Back cover: AP/WWP

EDITORIAL		*ART*	
Managing Editor:	Jeff Mahony	Creative Director:	Joe T. Nguyen
Associate Editors:	Melissa A. Bennett	Assistant Art Director:	Lance Doyle
	Gia C. Manalio	Senior Graphic Designers:	Marla B. Gladstone
	Mike Micciulla		Susannah C. Judd
	Paula Stuckart		David S. Maloney
Assistant Editors:	Heather N. Carreiro		Carole Mattia-Slater
	Jennifer Renk		David Ten Eyck
	Joan C. Wheal	Graphic Designers:	Jennifer J. Bennett
Editorial Assistants:	Timothy R. Affleck		Sean-Ryan Dudley
	Beth Hackett		Kimberly Eastman
	Christina M. Sette		Melani Gonzalez
	Steven Shinkaruk		Jim MacLeod
			Jeremy Maendel
PRODUCTION			Chery-Ann Poudrier
Production Manager:	Scott Sierakowski		
		R&D	
		Product Development Manager:	Paul Rasid

ISBN 1-58598-166-4

306 Industrial Park Road
Middletown, CT 06457
www.CheckerBee.com

Table Of Contents

Meet Jeff Gordon®

Jeff Gordon possesses one of the most recognizable faces in NASCAR and drives one of its best-known cars. But what else do you know about the Winston Cup phenomenon with fiery desire and a refuse-to-lose attitude?

Jeff Gordon is the forerunner of the new age of NASCAR. Young, handsome, clean-cut and media-savvy, Gordon brings to NASCAR a flair for winning and a talent to promote himself, his sport and his sponsors.

From an in-depth biography to a win-by-win accounting of Gordon's many track triumphs, the CheckerBee Fan Guide™ to Jeff Gordon® will bring the world of Jeff Gordon straight to you. What tracks does Gordon prefer to race on? Who are his chief competitors? Those questions and more are answered within these pages.

If you're new to racing, a look at some of NASCAR's legendary drivers will help you put Gordon's many successes into perspective, and "Race Day Experience" and "Life Behind The Wheel" will give you dramatic and pulse-raising examples of what it's like to attend a race and what it feels like when Gordon is piloting his No. 24 DuPont Chevy Monte Carlo to Victory Lane! We also give you an "anatomy" course on a race car, and introduce you to the 23 NASCAR racetracks around the country.

Gordon has driven many cars during his 10-year NASCAR career, and we've got them featured here. We've also showcased some of the many items of Gordon memorabilia you can acquire at the racetrack or the souvenir shop.

So don't waste your time spinning your wheels! The green flag is about to drop and the race is about to begin! Turn the page now and enter the world of Jeff Gordon!

THE WONDER BOY

Tracking A Champion: A Jeff Gordon® Biography

There are two kinds of people in the world – talkers and doers – and you know which one Jeff Gordon is! He's been "doing it" on NASCAR's toughest tracks for 10 years, beating the best, thrilling fans and winning Winston Cup championships. To his many loyal fans, No. 24 isn't *one* of the best – he *is* the best, period.

You'd think an athlete with good manners, a big heart and tons of ability would be universally loved, but Jeff Gordon can't shake that "Wonder Boy" label he earned as a hotshot, 21-year-old rookie. Some fans see that clean-cut image and think he was born with a silver spoon in his mouth. Well, forget the silver spoon – Gordon was born with a steering wheel in his hands!

Gordon's Green Flag

Gordon was born on August 4, 1971, in Vallejo, California. He was the second of two children born to Will and Carol Gordon (he has an older sister, Kim), but his parents divorced when he was still very young. Little did anyone know then what greatness would come from those beginnings!

Jeff Gordon holds up his third Winston Cup trophy on November 8, 1998.

Gordon got his first up-close look at the racing world at Vallejo Speedway, but he probably doesn't remember it! He was only 1 year old when he made his first trip there – tagging along with Kim on his mom's first date with a racing enthusiast named John Bickford. By all accounts, it was a good night. Not only did John and Carol marry a couple of years later, but it also marked the beginning of a relationship that would put Gordon in the driver's seat for good.

It was Bickford who raised young Gordon with an appreciation for racing in all forms. He nurtured the boy's need for speed by giving him a BMX bike, which Gordon promptly started racing around the neighborhood. You can imagine what the neighbors must have thought! "I liked everything that went fast at that age," Gordon once told Larry King. On that point, Gordon wasn't much different from a lot of kids, but it wasn't long before he set himself apart.

By the time he was 5 years old, Gordon was practicing laps in a quarter midget car Bickford had purchased for him. "We'd take that car out every night after I got home from work and run it lap after lap," Bickford once said. "Jeff couldn't seem to get enough of it."

Gordon acknowledges the fans at Atlanta Motor Speedway
before the start of the NAPA 500 in 1998.

With the encouragement of his parents, Gordon really took to the car. "I had no idea what I was getting myself into," Gordon recalled. "I just found something that I enjoyed, and they really pushed me into that career."

Mighty Midget

Gordon reflects on the competition (Bill Elliott) before the start of the Daytona 500 in 2001.

APWWP

At the tender age of 8, Gordon was almost unbeatable in the quarter midget races. In 1979, he won his first national championship in the quarter midget division. He would go on to capture two more national quarter midget championships, as well as four national go-kart class championships. He regularly beat kids his own age, and even older kids, much to their parents' dismay!

Although Gordon enjoyed racing success at a young age, life wasn't always easy for him. Critics talk about Gordon now as if he were born into a family of wealth and privilege, as if he "had it easy" growing up. Nothing could be further from the truth. Bickford says that Gordon's critics "have no idea about Jeff sleeping in the back of his truck, because he couldn't drive the diesel down the freeway, about making belly pans [a device that prevents a vehicle from becoming airborne] and selling them at the racetrack because we were holding on to every dime." His hard work and sacrifice as a youngster, however, would pay off big dividends years later.

Jeff Gordon On His 2000 Season

"I think that it was one of those years where we learned a lot about ourselves, and there were frustrating times. But I think that is what's made us stronger and the team that we are today."

On The Move

When Gordon was in his early teens, his family moved to Pittsboro, Indiana, not far from Indianapolis. The move to Indiana was the ultimate unselfish move, for his parents knew that their son had special ability and that he could really develop as a driver in the cradle of midget racing, the Midwest. This was no small sacrifice, as Bickford gave up his California manufacturing business. But in Indiana, Gordon would be able to race open-wheel cars and compete against adults, which he couldn't do in California because of age restrictions.

When Gordon turned 16 in 1987, he earned his racing license from the United States Auto Club (USAC), the youngest driver ever to do so. In 1989, he made all those laps in the backyard as a kid worth it when he won the USAC Midget Rookie of the Year award. It was a heady year for Gordon – he not only graduated from high school, but spent time racing in Australia and New Zealand! By this time, he was familiar with the racer's lifestyle – packing up and spending weekends racing on tracks all over the country.

Looking back on these early days, Gordon knows they were an important part of his future success as a driver. "I think [what] got me to this level is starting at a young age and yes, having some natural ability," he told Larry

Craig Jones/ALLSPORT

Gordon passes Rusty Wallace during the Goodwrench 400
at North Carolina Speedway on February 22, 1998.

King. "But then, all those years of experience of racing on all these different tracks all over the country, in Australia, New Zealand – I have been all over the world racing. And I think all that experience has really gotten me to this level and helped me to excel."

In 1990, Gordon won the USAC Midget Series National Championship, becoming the youngest Midget Class champion ever, at age 19. He followed that up the next year by becoming the youngest USAC Silver Crown Division National champion. As amazing as these achievements were, success on the midget circuit was one thing. But stock cars? That was something else!

Head For The Mountains (Of Busch)

Once again, John Bickford helped his stepson along with his budding racing career by suggesting that he attend NASCAR legend Buck Baker's driving school in Rockingham, North Carolina. It was a strange arrangement: ESPN came to the school to shoot a special feature on Gordon, who was beginning to make a national name for himself on the sprint car circuit. In exchange for the publicity, the school let Gordon attend for free!

Under Baker's tutelage, Gordon took his first whack at stock car racing – and fell in love with it. Within a year, he had reached stock car racing's national stage in the Busch Grand National Division. Car owner Bill Davis immediately

APWWP

Gordon shows his trophy for winning the pole at the Coca-Cola 600 in 1998.

recognized Gordon's superior skills and signed him up to drive his No. 1 Ford, first sponsored by Outback Steakhouse, then later by Carolina Ford Dealers and Baby Ruth.

In 1991, Gordon's first season of Busch series racing, he racked up five top-five finishes and raced to the Rookie of the Year award. He showed no signs of slowing down in 1992, when he won an incredible 11 pole positions. After only two years on the Busch circuit, Gordon proved he was ready to race with the big boys.

Winston Cup Bound

In 1992, Winston Cup series car owner Rick Hendrick watched Gordon win a frantic race at Atlanta Motor Speedway. Gordon's poise and what some would call "calculated recklessness" convinced Hendrick that he was watching a superstar in the making. Soon after, Gordon signed a contract to race for Hendrick Motorsports on the Winston Cup series circuit. It marked the end of his working relationship with Bill Davis and the start of an amazing Winston Cup ride.

Though Gordon got a taste of NASCAR's premier circuit in 1992 – he started the last race at Atlanta Motor Speedway in 1992 and failed to finish it

ALLSPORT/ALLSPORT

Gordon checks his car to ensure that everything is
working properly before a race in 1993.

– he made a real splash the following year. It was a learning process for the rookie, but he figured things out quickly. His great rookie performance in 1993 included two second-place finishes and

Gordon On Keeping The Faith

"I think the only way for me, my wife, my family, really our entire race team to get through what goes on out there, is to put our faith in God, know it's in His hands."

seven top-five finishes. When all was said and done, the 22-year-old Gordon cruised to the Winston Cup Rookie of the Year award, and was saddled with a nickname that was both complimentary and sarcastic: "Wonder Boy." His achievements were incredible, but many scoffed at the notion of such a young man being able to attain them.

The Sweetest Victory Of All

Perhaps Gordon's greatest "victory" of the 1993 season was meeting model Brooke Sealy at the qualifiying races for the Daytona 500, the very first race of the year. Brooke was the reigning Miss Winston and when the two met, the sparks flew. "He stole the trophy that day to become the youngest winner of that race ever," Brooke recalled in an interview. "And . . . little did he know it, but that day he also stole my heart."

Gordon and his wife, Brooke, watch the qualifying heats for the DieHard 500 in 1995.

Jamie Squire/Allsport

There was only one problem. It's an unwritten rule in NASCAR that drivers are not to get romantically involved with Miss Winstons. But Jeff and Brooke felt they had something special, so they carried on their romance in secret. As he told Larry King: "So you know, us guys that are out there competing every weekend, we don't get a chance to get around and meet too many nice girls. So when one comes along, even if she's working in the sport, you are going to take advantage of it, and we just clicked right away." Today, Gordon and his wife are the most recognizable and popular couple in racing.

"Refuse To Lose"

After Gordon's Rookie of the Year campaign, the pressure was on for him to prove that he was the "real thing" and not a flash in the oil pan – and he was up to the challenge. He got his first Winston Cup series win at the Coca-Cola 600 at Charlotte Motor Speedway, the same race he'd finished second in the year before.

> ### Down To Earth
>
> Of his celebrity status, Gordon said in a 1998 interview, "Success feels real good, but really, I don't think of myself as being famous or a celebrity. I happen to be a race car driver with success."

But his second win was even more special. In front of a loyal hometown crowd, Gordon beat Ernie Irvan to take the inaugural Brickyard 400 at Indianapolis Motor Speedway. Just three years removed from Indiana's midget circuit, Gordon had returned as a Winston Cup series winner! In his second full

David Taylor/ALLSPORT

Gordon's ready to race during Speedweek at Daytona International Speedway in 1999.

Winston Cup season, Gordon finished eighth in the final standings with 3,776 points, and earned more than $1 million for the first time in his career. But the best was yet to come!

Gordon got off to a fast start in 1995, winning three out of the first six races. At the end of a grueling season, he had silenced his critics by edging out his rival, the "Intimidator" Dale Earnhardt, by 34 points for his first Winston Cup Series championship. In only his third year on the circuit, Gordon had proved that he could not only hold his own against NASCAR's best, but he could beat them, too!

All was not roses, however. He suffered a bit of a setback in 1996; despite posting 10 wins, he struggled through adversity all year, including a cut tire at the Brickyard 400 and a wreck at Talladega. But Gordon showed his resilience the next year, when he became the youngest driver to win the Daytona 500. He also won the Winston Million, thanks to winning three of

four "crown jewel" Winston Cup series races. Once again, Gordon won 10 races – but this time it was good enough to propel him to his second Winston Cup series championship, by a mere 14 points over Dale Jarrett.

AP/WWP

Bull's-Eye On His Back

With two champi-onships in three years, Gordon was no longer viewed as a baby-faced rookie – he was a marked man! Undaunted, he blew away the field, winning an amazing 13 races and cruising to yet another Winston Cup series

Gordon is all smiles away from the track in this photo taken in New York City in 1995.

Proving Ground

Gordon's had some ups and downs in his NASCAR career. What does he think it takes to earn respect in Winston Cup racing? "Winning championships, not winning championships, struggling, having to build this team back, to get back up on top." With his experience, Gordon should be the most respected driver in NASCAR!

championship by 364 points over Mark Martin. His stellar 1998 season made him NASCAR's biggest star. He also won the "No Bull 5" prize of $1 million twice – a little icing on the cake and part of the astounding $6 million he earned in purses that year.

With so much success on the track, it seemed natural for Gordon to take a stab at the business side of racing. Along with then–crew chief Ray Evernham, Gordon launched a Busch series racing team. One gets the sense that when Gordon does decide to hang up his helmet, he'll remain very active as a team owner. "I really have enjoyed the business side of racing," he has said. "I'm fortunate enough now where I'm a part owner of my race team, and so I would love to be more involved with that."

Trouble In Paradise?

Gordon's ride to the top of the NASCAR world seemed to hit a wall in 1999. His quest for a fourth Winston Cup series championship was derailed early when five members of his famous pit crew, the "Rainbow Warriors," left the Hendrick team for the rival Robert Yates Racing team.

Then, crew chief Ray Evernham resigned his position, essentially break

Gordon takes the checkered flag at the Pepsi 400 at Michigan International Speedway in 1998.

ing up a winning team. Although Gordon won the next two races after Evernham's departure under the direction of interim crew chief (now team manager) Brian Whitesell, he ended up with a mediocre year – by his high standards – limping into sixth in the final standings. It was a dose of reality for Gordon, who has never forgotten the importance of teamwork and has described racing as "a total team sport."

The pit crew gets to work during the California 500
at California Speedway in 1999.

Back On The Winning Track

Teamwork definitely was on Gordon's mind heading into the 2000 season, which he has called a "rebuilding year." He finished ninth in the final standings, but Gordon felt his new team was finding its footing. He told Larry King that "it was nice to go out there and show those who maybe didn't believe in us that it just takes time, and that we are still capable of winning races and championships."

Despite his up-and-down year on the track in 2000, Gordon reached the 50 career-win plateau. He also had success off the track, signing a lifetime agreement with Hendrick Motorsports and inking a new deal with primary sponsor DuPont that lasts through 2006.

And if the determination Gordon showed at the 2001 The Winston all-star race is any indication, he'll be back on top in no time! He won the race in amazing fashion when, on a rainy night, he got involved in a multi-car wreck only to jump into his backup car (after a rain delay) and blow away the competition for his third The Winston event win.

AP/WWP

Gordon is helped out of his car after a crash at The Winston at Lowe's Motor Speedway in 2001. The race would later be restarted, and Gordon would take the victory.

"Makeup!"

As one of the most popular and successful drivers in NASCAR, Gordon is as much in demand off the track as he is on it. In the new era of the sport, he's become a familiar and recognizable face in ads for toothpaste and for his secondary race sponsor, Pepsi. And then there were the "Got milk?" ads, in which he promoted one of his favorite drinks.

Over the years, loyal supporters have caught the driver of the No. 24 car on "Larry King Live," "The Tonight Show" and "The Late Show With David Letterman." Always willing to mingle with fans, Gordon actually answered phones in the ticket office of Chicagoland Speedway earlier this year! He's

You Can Say That Again

Gordon has said, "Once I do find something that I like, and that I'm pretty good at, I find ways to get better and better at it." Truer words were never spoken!

also appeared on "Spin City" and a made-for-TV racing movie called "Steel Chariots" – as himself, of course.

In January 2001, Gordon rode shotgun next to Regis Philbin as guest co-host of the "Live With Regis" show. He made another appearance on the show as part of a segment called "Mom's Dream Comes True." Gordon visited a big fan and surprised her with race tickets, a hat and other goodies. He took a similar gig for a CBS special called "Surprise, Surprise, Surprise!," hosted by Kathie Lee Gifford.

Boos? No Way!

If you can say anything at all about NASCAR fans, it's that they're extremely loyal and passionate about their racetrack heroes. They also have strong feelings for "the enemy," whomever driver that may be! With the exception of the late, great Dale Earnhardt, no other driver generates the raw emotion Gordon does. People either love him or hate him!

Why can't he seem to win some fans over? One reason is that he's become a mega-star in every sense of the word, and some fans don't care for that. For many fans, Gordon is the poster boy for NASCAR's new big-money, corporate image, the antithesis of NASCAR's rough-and-tumble, earthy roots. The fact that he was selected as one of the world's 50 most beautiful people by *PEOPLE* magazine hasn't helped any!

Jon Ferrey/ALLSPORT

Gordon is relaxed and ready to go at 1999's Kmart 400 at Michigan Speedway.

But some fans dislike Gordon simply because he's so good and has achieved so much success at a young age. In a 1999 *Florida Times-Union* article, Darrell Waltrip said, "Fans always hate to see the new guys come in and beat their heroes. When that happens, they usually respond in various ways, some of which you don't like."

Gordon knows the negative things that people say about him and sees how some people react to him at the track. Of the boos, he once said, "You know, hey, I understand it. If a guy's out there winning a bunch of races, you always pull for the underdog. Heck, I'm always pulling for the underdogs in any sport I watch, too." Success can breed popularity, but it can also breed boo-birds!

Not About The Money

Contrary to what some people might believe, with Gordon it's definitely not all about the money. Unlike many high-salaried athletes, he has a real sense of responsibility that extends beyond his family.

He and Brooke are extremely active in charity work, particularly through The Jeff Gordon Foundation. This organization supports children's charities like the Make-A-Wish Foundation, the Marrow Foundation and the Leukemia

David Taylor/Allsport

Gordon's motorcycle matches his rainbow-themed Chevrolet Monte Carlo and racing uniform. This photo was taken at Sears Point Raceway in 1999.

& Lymphoma Society. In addition to public appearances, Gordon raises money for charity by auctioning off rare items on the foundation's website, such as the cap he wore after winning The Winston in 2001 – signed by Gordon himself, of course. He also donated $100,000 of his "Winston Million" to the Marrow Foundation.

His religious beliefs are also firm. Thanks in part to Brooke's commitment to her faith, Gordon is a born-again Christian. Like many people of faith, he sees God at work in all aspects of his family and racing life: "I'm very blessed to have the life that I've had, and to go through all the different things I've gone through – ups and downs in this sport," he once said. "I have had some incredible success, but I've been through some nasty wrecks and have come out with no injuries. So I certainly thank God for that each and every day." With his faith in one pocket and his driving skill in the other, who knows what heights he will reach – on the Winston Cup circuit and in life!

Gordon signs a helmet for a fan at Lowe's Motor Speedway in 2000.

Gordon's Tales

From famous celebrities to regular folks, it seems like everybody has a story to tell about Jeff Gordon. The popularity, good humor and sincerity of the remarkable driver are evident in each of these memorable anecdotes.

The Price Is Right

Jeff Gordon has appeared several times on the QVC network to help sell his racing products, but the modest racer is surprised at how devoted his fans and collectors are. For his February 1999 appearance on the cable shopping network, about 2,000 people showed up for a live, remote broadcast from the All-American SportPark in Las Vegas. "It just blows me away when I see 2,000 people from this area out there just going crazy. You think you only see that in the Southeast [but] I'll tell you, I would probably have to argue that I probably wouldn't draw that many people in the Southeast at a place like that," Gordon said. Jeff Gordon might be surprised by his astounding popularity, but it's no secret to his fans – wherever they are!

Gordon has also used his time in front of the QVC cameras to show off

David Taylor/Allsport

Jeff Gordon wore his Pepsi racing suit when he raced at Las Vegas Motor Speedway in 1999.

his humor and rapport with the host and audience. In August 1997, when introduced as one of *PEOPLE* magazine's "50 Most Beautiful People," the self-deprecating Gordon said, "Voted by who, that's what I'm trying to figure out!" Former crew chief Ray Evernham didn't lack comedic timing – he quipped that he had been 51st on the list!

The King And The Honcho

Richard Petty is known as the "King" of NASCAR.

The death of Dale Earnhardt left an absence in the world of stock car racing. While no driver will ever take the Intimidator's place in the hearts of fans, shortly after Earnhardt's death, Richard Petty, the "King" of NASCAR, said that Gordon will be the driver to best step up and lead the sport out of one of its darkest hours.

NASCAR has always had a dominant driver leading the pack and forcing the other drivers to rise to the challenge. "I took [NASCAR] from one level and put it in another level," Petty said. "Earnhardt picked it up from there.. Petty indicates that Gordon is the next in line to carry that ability and responsibility. "To me, Gordon is the head honcho," he summed up. And with over 50 wins to his credit, Gordon is more than a quarter of the way to matching the King's record of 200 Winston Cup victories.

Kyle Petty, son of the King, has made statements that echo his father's. "Jeff does stand a chance to

Richard's Remarks

Richard Petty knew that the fans who loved Dale Earnhardt hated Jeff Gordon, and vice versa. "The people that didn't like Earnhardt or his ways of doing things, they could go with Gordon" because Gordon is the smooth part of everything that was the rough part about Earnhardt," Petty said.

dominate like the King did, for a longer period of time," said the younger Petty. "Jeff Gordon is the next big thing that has helped the sport grow in the last four or five years, more so than anything else."

Jonathan Ferrey/ALLSPORT

Richard (left) and Kyle Petty pose behind their Petty Enterprises Dodge Intrepid at the California Speedway in 2001.

The Road To Recovery

Athletes are often admired for the successes they achieve within their sport. Gordon deserves high marks for his actions off the track, as well, for his efforts in helping to spread the word about North Carolina's "Booze It & Lose It" campaign designed to combat drunk drivers.

"Christopher," a young racing fan, lay comatose for days after being trapped in his father's van for hours when a drunk driver struck the vehicle. The boy, a devoted Gordon fan, had a life-size poster of the DuPont driver in his hospital room to aid in his recovery. Gordon was told of Christopher's condition and sent him an autographed picture and die-cast replicas of his No. 24 Monte Carlo. "I send my best wishes to Christopher and his family," Gordon said, "and am proud to be part of 'Booze It & Lose It.' I commend law enforcement for all they do and the challenges they face," said Gordon.

Hero Of The Highways

Highway drivers who dream that they are behind the wheel of the No. 24 Chevy Monte Carlo had better not try to drive as fast as Jeff Gordon in Pittsboro, Indiana – even though Gordon has a road there named in his honor!

Gordon was honored by his hometown of Pittsboro in 1999 when County Road 275 East was renamed Jeff Gordon Boulevard. "It's unbelievable the way my old friends and the whole town of Pittsboro have supported me. They've been there since the beginning of my professional racing career and have followed me ever since," wrote Gordon on his website. What an incredible feeling it is to have the whole town come together to make me a permanent part of the community. I'm honored."

Chris Stanford/Allsport

Don't be surprised if you see this car cruising down Jeff Gordon Boulevard in Pittsboro, Indiana!

Although born in California, Gordon's stepfather moved the family to Indiana where young Jeff could compete in races without age restrictions, and Jeff considers Pittsboro to be his hometown.

Taking It On The Chin

As host of "The Tonight Show," Jay Leno hobnobs with celebrities, musicians and comedians each night. It might come as something of a surprise, therefore, that the popular host was picked to drive the pace car at the 2001 Brickyard 400. But Leno, a classic car buff and occasional celebrity racer, is as comfortable behind a steering wheel as he is behind his "Tonight Show" desk.

In preparation for his racing duties, Leno met with Gordon at the Indianapolis Motor Speedway. "Jeff's a nice guy and a great NASCAR driver, but, boy, he needs some help in the joke department. I had hoped to give him a tip or two on driving this track, but like a good student, I listened to his advice," joked Leno.

Call Him A Role Model

In his years on the court, basketball star Charles Barkley was a dominant force who earned a reputation of being a tough competitor who wasn't afraid to speak his mind off the court. Barkley's personality might clash with Gordon's image as a friendly role model, but the two athletes reported-

Jay Leno (left) gets some driving tips from Gordon on the straightaway at Indianapolis Motor Speedway in 2001.

ly hit it off on their first meeting. "When I was growing up, everybody hated the Celtics because they always won," Barkley said. "Jeff Gordon is going through that same thing. When you think about it, there is no way possible that any person in the entire world should dislike him. What has he ever done except win? He's never in trouble, he's very religious, and he's always kicking butt. What more would you want in an athlete?"

Jeff's Top Ten

It's no secret that late-night talk show host David Letterman is a big fan of fast cars, but did you know that Gordon is a big fan of David Letterman? "I guess since I was probably about 15 years old, I thought that if I made it on 'David Letterman,' that would be it. And then it happened," said Gordon.

Gordon has gone on to make several appearances on Letterman's show and even helped out Letterman on February 15, 1999, by reading the night's top ten list – "The Top Ten Thoughts That Cross Your Mind When Driving 200 MPH."

10. *Oh my god, the bag of groceries is still on the roof.*

9. *Wonder if I could make it over to Wendy's drive-thru and back and still win?*

Gordon was thrilled when he made an appearance on David Letterman's television show.

8. *Just a little bit faster, and I'll be home in time for "Felicity."*

7. *Lap 168 – yeah, this isn't getting old.*

6. *In the words of the great Winston Churchill, "I'm haulin' tail now, sister!"*

5. *Oh great, the only tape I have is Lionel Richie.*

4. *Why is my pit crew charging me $1.35 a gallon?*

3. *Tie-fighters, nine o'clock! Punch it, Chewie!*

2. *This is still safer than riding in a New York City cab.*

1. *Gee, maybe I shouldn't have had all that Nyquil.*

The Crusader

Through personal appearances and trackside heroics, Gordon has had the privilege of touching the hearts of millions of fans. In June of 1999, Gordon had an opportunity to touch more than his fans' hearts – he touched their souls.

Gordon, who finds strength in his Christian faith, had an opportunity to speak in front of tens of thousands of people at the RCA Dome in Indianapolis as part of a Billy Graham crusade. "The greatest thing that has happened to me is my relationship with Jesus Christ," Gordon told the audience. "Racing is still very important to me, and it is one of my priorities, but it is certainly not at the top. God is at the top, my wife and my family come below that and racing comes after that."

After the event was over, Gordon had high praise for Rev. Graham. "I really enjoyed it. Just meeting Billy Graham was quite an honor. He's been such an influence and touched so many people's hearts and been a part of their lives," said Gordon. "To be able to meet somebody like that who has that kind of influence, it was awesome."

AP/WWP

Gordon, Terry Labonte (No. 5) and Ricky Craven (No. 25) were teammates when they achieved this 1-2-3 finish at the Daytona 500 in 1997.

Fast Friends

Stock car racing doesn't leave a lot of room for friendships between racers. When a race comes down to the wire, two drivers who consider each other "friends" may do ugly things to each other in an attempt to take the checkered flag.

Gordon and Ricky Craven are the exception – two drivers who share a genuine friendship. "I was asked about my best friend in racing, and I said Ricky Craven. It goes back to the early days of being together," said Gordon during a NASCAR.com on-line chat.

Those feelings of friendship are reciprocated by Craven, who was a teammate of Gordon's when Craven raced for Hendrick Motorsports. Even after Craven left the Hendrick stable, he remained friends with Gordon. When Craven won his first pole after post-concussion syndrome kept him on the sidelines for months, Craven said, "[T]he first guy to get to me was Jeff Gordon. I saw him running out of his trailer as I was pulling in. He pulled the net down and gave me a big hug. That was like the world had been lifted off my shoulders."

Craven and Gordon talk before the start of the New England 300 in 2000.

Keeping Up With The Gordons

The life of a NASCAR driver is hectic and non-stop. There are appearances to make, business commitments to be kept, testing sessions to be conducted and much more. Even on his "days off," Jeff Gordon has little time for rest and relaxation. Think you can keep up with him? Read on and find out.

AP/WWP

Gordon tries to accommodate as many autograph seekers as he can. He's pictured here at the Daytona International Speedway in June of 2000.

You might think that race days are the only time you can catch Jeff Gordon on television. Well, you'd be mistaken. In fact, in the first five months of 2001 alone, Gordon appeared as Regis Philbin's co-host on "Live With Regis," came back again to appear with Philbin and his co-host, Kelly Ripa, and was interviewed twice on "Larry King Live" – once with other drivers and a second time alone.

As one of the hottest drivers on the Winston Cup circuit, Gordon is in demand both on and off the track. As a matter of fact, CNN talk show host Larry King told Gordon that if he wasn't a racer, he could have a great career in front of the camera!

The Next Regis Philbin?

Gordon does indeed seem to have an enjoyable time during his television appearances. When he co-hosted with Philbin on January 15, 2001, Gordon allowed Philbin and New York spa owner Marcia Kilgore to give him a rose petal and cucumber facial. We bet he got some ribbing from his NASCAR buddies about that!

Gordon also appeared on the May 11, 2001, "Mom's Dream Comes True" segment of "Live With Regis And Kelly." He surprised a fan whose daughter had written to the show that her mother was " . . . the world's biggest Jeff Gordon fan." That's a Mother's Day surprise that woman won't soon forget!

In addition to the great publicity for himself and NASCAR (and of course to the delight of his fans), Gordon uses his appearances as a means to promote the important work he does with the Jeff Gordon Foundation, a charitable organization that he and his wife Brooke founded in 1999. For example, he used the January "Live With Regis" appearance to plug the foundation, saying in an on-line chat, "It was a great opportunity for me and it was great to

AP/WWP

Gordon meets the press in January of 2001 at Hendrick Motorsports headquarters in Harrisburg, North Carolina.

AP/WWP

Jeff Gordon and his wife Brooke celebrate his victory at the Pennsylvania 500 in 1998.

promote the Jeff Gordon Foundation. Brooke and I are both behind it a lot this year, helping to get awareness up for the Marrow Foundation and Leukemia Foundation. There were some embarrassing moments but you have to go into it willing to have fun and enjoy yourself, and I did." Hmmm, he couldn't be talking about the facial episode, could he?

All For A Good Cause

Besides his television appearances, Gordon also keeps quite busy with his charitable work. The Jeff Gordon Foundation primarily supports three organizations – The Leukemia & Lymphoma Society, The Make-A-Wish Foundation and The Marrow Foundation. The Jeff Gordon Foundation also supports various other charities on a case-by-case basis. Gordon often meets with children from the Make-A-Wish Foundation before races, something that is never easy, but which he nevertheless does with grace and compassion.

The Jeff Gordon Foundation also frequently holds on-line auctions to raise money for charity. Gordon revealed in an on-line chat in the spring of 2001 that the foundation plans to auction off a special edition die-cast car, the profits of which will go to the Jeff Gordon Foundation to benefit its favorite charities.

Too Much Is Never Enough

Gordon is a video game junkie whose favorite games include "Grand Turismo," "NASCAR 2001" and "Super Cross." Doesn't he ever get enough of racing?

Public Life, Private Person

All of this might be enough to wear a normal person out, but, then again, Jeff Gordon is not your average person. When he does have downtime, however, Gordon enjoys spending it with his wife, Brooke, a former Miss Winston. He makes sure that he takes every Monday off to spend time with her. Gordon says, "I'll spend the whole day with Brooke and try to stay as far away from racing as possible. Sometimes we won't talk or even think about the race coming up or the one we've just run."

Time away from his duties as a Winston Cup star is essential to Gordon. Fans are important to him, and to that end he makes a lot of time for appearances and autograph sessions. But although Gordon is gracious to fans and appreciates their support, being in the spotlight can take its toll.

For example, Gordon and his wife used to live by Lake Norman near Charlotte, North Carolina, an area where many NASCAR stars live. They often had fans show up at their house. It's been reported that some fans would sit in their cars and stare, while others would even come up and knock on the door. Gordon has recalled, "We constantly had people going by and taking pictures. You couldn't walk in front of a window at night. It was like, if we were gonna play on the boat, we had to get everything ready." At those times, Gordon would look at his wife and ask, "Ready?" "Ready,"

AP-WWP

Jeff and Brooke Gordon show who's number one after his win at the DieHard 500 at Talladega in April, 2000.

Brooke would reply, and they'd grab their gear and race to the boat, hoping that nobody had seen them.

It was partially because of this constant exposure that the Gordons moved to Florida, where they wouldn't be as recognizable. In a 1999 interview with the *Charlotte Observer,* Gordon said, " . . . when we're there we're able to get away and relax. You're able to eat and enjoy a nice evening out." Gordon was a little worried that the move would mean too much time spent away from the DuPont team's race shop near Charlotte, but said that if he doesn't have "time with Brooke and to get away on my boat or to the movies, I won't be as mentally sharp on race day."

Rules Of The Road

In 1999, Gordon appeared on *Good Morning America* as the instructor for the show's five-part driving safety series, "The Great American Driving Test."

The privacy that Florida allows the Gordons won out over any concerns that Gordon may have had about the move. The two still keep a home in North Carolina, however, where they are able to occasionally enjoy quiet evenings out. Gordon told a reporter, "You just have to know where to go" to avoid being recognized in that state.

At Daytona International Speedway in February, 1999, Gordon slides into his car as a member of his team and Brooke look on.

She's The Inspiration

Jeff and Brooke Gordon are one of NASCAR's true love stories. In fact, on his website, *www.jeffgordon.com,* Gordon cites her as his greatest inspiration in life. Brooke travels with him to every race on the couple's Lear jet, which they use to fly to races and appearances.

When they can, the couple enjoys dining out together and going to movies. They usually arrive in the city where Gordon will be racing on the Thursday before the race. Their routine is to go out to dinner together and then to a movie if it's not too late. Saturday nights they have a regular Bible study group with some of the other NASCAR drivers and their wives. When there's an off weekend, Gordon

Brooke and Jeff celebrate the second win of his career at the Brickyard in 1994.

says, "I'll mark days off the calendar and set aside days where we can relax. But that's getting tougher and tougher because we'll have two more races [in 2001]. There are more demands."

Practicing What He Preaches

Being such a public figure, you might think that Gordon would have to watch himself carefully when he's out and about as a private citizen, but he doesn't worry about that much. When asked by a reporter if he can say what he wants and drink what he wants in public, Gordon responded, "I do the same things at home. I mean, it's no different. I don't like to swear at any time. I don't drink – much. I mean, yeah, on occasion I might have a beer or a glass of wine or something like that. So when I'm out in public I don't really have to change that. I pretty much live what I preach."

Craig Jones/Allsport

Jeff shows off Brooke and his trophy for winning the Mountain Dew Southern 500 at Darlington in 1997.

The best part of the off-season for Gordon is relaxing and spending time with his family. He and Brooke might go out on their boat – or go scuba diving, one of Gordon's favorite activities. They might relax at home with some prime-time television. Gordon enjoys watching *Friends, Who Wants To Be A Millionaire* and *Frasier.* Brooke may be partially responsible for this devotion to maintaining a normal life. She has said, "I try to balance his life because this racing business is so intense and your emotions are just on a roller coaster every week, and I try to let him know there's more to life than racing."

Even during the off-season, however, Jeff can't entirely get away from racing. He says, "Even when I'm in a street car, driving down the road, it's like I'm in a race car. Not speedwise. It's just that I'm constantly paying total attention to everything around me, constantly clocking myself from one point to the next."
Which is why he's the best.

Pretty Photogenic

Gordon was chosen as one of *PEOPLE* magazine's "50 Most Beautiful People" in 1998. He also wore the white milk mustache in a "Got Milk" ad.

The Other Side Of The Wall

With stock car races sometimes won or lost by a tenth of a second, it's often on pit road that a driver's fate is decided. Jeff Gordon's elite pit crew makes every second count in their hunt for another Winston Cup championship.

When Jeff Gordon hit an uncharacteristic dry spell in 1999 and 2000, starting 13 races without a victory, many looked to the departure of crew chief Ray Evernham and five of the Rainbow Warriors – Gordon's famous pit crew – as the reason.

Now with Gordon back at the top of his game, his success can be attributed to new crew chief Robbie Loomis and his revamped pit team. With the crew's blazing speed and fiery determination on pit road, their attitude fits the new fire-and-flames paint scheme on Gordon's famous No. 24 Chevrolet Monte Carlo perfectly.

The crew works to repair Gordon's car after a collision with Kenny Wallace at the Coca-Cola 600 at Lowe's Motor Speedway in May of 2001.

In The Pits

During every race, each car is assigned a pit box, where all car work is performed during a pit stop. The crew chief is responsible for deciding when (or when not) to pit the car. If the driver pits too early, precious time and track positioning might be lost. If the driver pits too late, the car runs the risk of running out of gas or wearing out its tires. The pit crew monitors the race action from the adjoining pit stall. When Gordon pulls into the pit, the crew jumps over the wall and immediately gets to work.

Gordon's crew is famous for its lightning-quick pit stops. Tires are handed off to the tire changer, who secures the new Goodyears by tightening the lug nuts with an air wrench. The car, which was jacked up by the jack man, is dropped to the asphalt – ready for action. Before Gordon exits the pit, he may get a quick drink or his windshield wiped off, all of which is done with a large pole from the other side of the wall. Also on the "other side" are additional members of the pit crew such as scorers and and video technicians.

A pole extends from over the wall (at right) to wash Gordon's windshield as the team speeds to service his car at Rockingham at the Dura Lube/Big Kmart 400 in 1999.

Gordon can't just roar out of the pit and back into the action – speeds are monitored on pit road in the interest of safety. But once he's back on track, it's back to speeds of nearly 200 miles per hour as Gordon's Chevy blows by any Dodge, Ford, Pontiac or rival Chevy in its path.

Hail To The Chief

Crew chief Robbie Loomis is the man who makes the important decisions concerning race-track tactics. He joined Gordon's team at the start of the 2000 season. Prior to his involvement with Hendrick Motorsports (the business that owns Gordon's racing team), Loomis was crew chief for Petty Enterprises.

Gordon and crew chief Robbie Loomis (right) have lots to smile about after winning the Save Mart/Kragen 350 at Sears Point in 2000.

Although his first win with Gordon didn't occur until April 16, 2000, from that point on Loomis showed his strengths, helping Gordon score nine top-10 finishes in his last 10 races of the season.

Loomis is optimistic that an even better season is just around the corner. In a recent interview he said, "There's been a lot of areas that we've improved in. Our bodies are a lot better. Our engines are a lot better. We've got a lot of new personnel. But I think the big thing is just togetherness. The guys have really stuck together even through our rough times and our rough races. We've come back."

Before Loomis took the reins from the departed Evernham, now–team manager Brian Whitesell served as interim crew chief. He's been with Hendrick Motorsports since its inception in 1984 (for more on Hendrick Motorsports, check out "The Hendrick Motorsports Team" on page 43). Whitesell guided the No. 24 car to back-to-back victories in his first two races as crew chief and was promoted to the position of team manager after the hiring of

Pitted Against Each Other

Regarded as the "Super Bowl" of pit crew events, the Unocal 76 Pit Crew Competition is held each year at North Carolina Speedway. Jeff Gordon's pit crew won the competition in 1994 with a then-record time of 19.363 seconds.

Loomis. With these two proven winners on Gordon's team, the No. 24 DuPont Chevy has a bright future ahead.

Robbie Loomis, left, points some things out to Gordon
at the Atlanta Motor Speedway in November of 2000.

Gas And Go

NASCAR rules allow for seven pit crew members to go "over the wall" at a time. This team usually consists of a jack man, two front tire changers, two rear tire changers, a gas man and a catch-can man. Spotters and driver-service professionals play a vital role from the other side of the wall, as well.

For Gordon to have a shot at winning, jackman Chris Anderson needs to get his car off the ground in a hurry – only one or two pumps of the jack is all he has time for! Shane Church, Craig Currione, Todd Gantt and Steve Letarte have the equally important responsibility of carrying and changing the front and rear tires. The pit crew's job has become so specialized that it shouldn't come as a surprise to learn that the tire carrier

Pit-O-Rama

The three Winston Cup racing teams that make up Hendrick Motorsports participate in a "pit-o-rama" to get ready for the upcoming NASCAR season. This mock event between the No. 5 (Terry Labonte), No. 24 and No. 25 (Jerry Nadeau) cars prepares the pit crews for the Daytona 500.

and the tire changer are two completely different jobs, and are the responsibility of separate individuals.

Gas man Jeff Craven and catch-can man Jason Burdett also hold jobs that are related in function, but require two men to perform. The gas man fills the car up using two 11-gallon canisters. Luckily, the gas man doesn't have to clear the pit wall with two cans in his hands. A second gas man waits behind the wall with a fresh canister to pass to his crew mate. The catch-can man collects any excess gas that may have spilled from the fuel cell.

The spotter doesn't go over the wall, but has an important role nonetheless. As Gordon's spotter, it's Ron Thiel's job to keep Gordon aware of track conditions and passing opportunities – something Gordon can't do when every ounce of his concentration is focused on getting to Victory Lane. Spotters sit in a location that gives them an unobstructed view of the whole track, and they communicate their observations directly to the driver.

Back at the race shop are specialized mechanics and fabricators who work behind the scenes to prepare Gordon's ride each week for its next Winston Cup competition.

The New Breed

Gordon's pit crew was one of the first to utilize and perfect new techniques – such as strength conditioning – that have since become the standard in the sport. These new pit crews more closely resemble professional athletic teams than automotive garage employees. While scaling a 28-inch wall might not seem like a strenuous activity, try performing that task with two tires or an 11-gallon gas can in your arms!

The pit crew is key to winning a race, and their efforts here will help Gordon win the 1998 Pepsi 400 at Daytona.

Hendrick Motorsports enlisted a pit crew coach to establish an exercise routine for the crew. "We do weight training, cardiovascular workouts, individual drills and full-team practices up to four days a week to get ready for race day," said coach Greg Miller, who has multiple degrees in exercise physiology.

Working in the pits provides a rush equal to the thrill experienced by the drivers. Pit road is a high-speed work zone where crew members must be on their toes to avoid the possibility of a broken leg, or worse. In 1990, a member of Bill Elliott's crew was killed in the pit after getting hit by Ricky Rudd's out-of-control car. Being in top physical shape reduces some of the risk inherent in navigating through the congestion of pit road, and Gordon's crew has what it takes to bring him to victory time and time again.

The crew works furiously during a pit stop at the Daytona 500 in February of 2001.

AP/WWP

The Hendrick Motorsports Team

What started as a one-car operation in 1984 is now home to some of the most popular and successful drivers in NASCAR. Now well into its second decade, Hendrick Motorsports remains a trendsetter in the ever-changing world of stock car racing.

Hendrick Motorsports is the vision of Joseph R. "Rick" Hendrick III, a man whose thirst for speed and desire to win has led to unprecedented success in the sport of stock car racing.

Hendrick Motorsports can boast that it is the only organization to field a Winston Cup champion four seasons in a row. From 1995 to 1998, Hendrick drivers took up permanent residence in Victory Lane as Jeff Gordon drove to the championship in 1995, 1997 and 1998, and teammate Terry Labonte won it in 1996. Hendrick has also succeeded in NASCAR's Craftsman Truck Series, where Jack Sprague is a two-time champion. Before the triumphs,

AP/WWP

Gordon and team owner Rick Hendrick share a laugh at a 1999 news conference announcing Gordon's partnership in the No. 24 team.

checkered flags and championships, however, Hendrick was involved with cars in a different way – he sold them! As he went from car dealer to race team owner, Hendrick built a NASCAR dynasty.

Building A Champion

Hendrick Motorsports has come a long way from its beginnings as a one-car team. Originally called "All-Star Racing," the early Hendrick Motorsports team included superstars Geoff Bodine, Tim Richmond and Darrell Waltrip. These legendary drivers of the 1980s provided the foundation for the championships of the 1990s.

A dynasty in action: Hendrick Motorsports teammates celebrate their 1-2-3 finish in the 1997 Daytona 500. Terry Labonte (left) came in second, Jeff Gordon (center) was first and Ricky Craven (right) finished third.

How does Hendrick do it? Many of the secrets of his success reside in the 65-acre Hendrick Motorsports racing complex in Harrisburg, North Carolina. Here, over 300 employees build the famous Hendrick stock cars, as well as hundreds of engines. Hendrick engines are so prized that the complex even makes engines that other teams can lease. But no matter how flawlessly a car is built, it can't race without a driver. Jeff Gordon may be the brightest jewel in the Hendrick crown, but the following drivers are also committed to bringing home championships to the Hendrick Motorsports family.

Ricky Hendrick

Ricky Hendrick is making his father proud as a young racer in the Craftsman Truck Series (he also puts in time in the Busch circuit). At 21, Hendrick has shown the poise of a veteran, recording multiple top-10 finishes behind the wheel of his Chevy Silverado. If all goes according to plan, he will be testing his prowess in the Winston Cup Series in the near future.

Terry Labonte at the 1999 Goody's 500 – his 625th consecutive Winston Cup race.

Terry Labonte

Considered the "Iron Man" of stock car racing for his 655 consecutive starts, Terry Labonte is eager to prove to Rick Hendrick that he has not become rusty in recent years. Labonte, older brother of 2000 Winston Cup champion Bobby Labonte, first won the Winston Cup championship in 1984 for owner Billy Hagan, and Hendrick had results like that in mind when he signed Labonte to a contract in 1994.

Labonte proved that with age comes experience, winning the Winston Cup championship for a second time in 1996. That same year, teammate Jeff Gordon finished second in the points standings, thanks to a season-high total of 10 victories.

No stranger to winning big races, Labonte also took the checkered flag at The Winston in 1988 and 1999. Could a third Winston Cup championship be around the corner?

Living In The Fast Lane

Rick Hendrick is one of just a handful of owners to race in a Winston Cup competition. In 1987 and 1988, Hendrick joined the elite company of such other owner-drivers as Richard Petty and Cale Yarborough when he sat behind the wheel for two races.

Jerry Nadeau

His hometown of Danbury, Connecticut, is far removed from the racing hotbeds of the South and Midwest, but Jerry Nadeau has successfully made the transition to the Winston Cup Series. Before his involvement in NASCAR's top circuit, Nadeau divided his time between the Busch Series and various open-wheel competitions. He then made the step up to the Winston Cup, joining the Hendrick team in 2000 after bouncing around four racing teams in just three seasons. Nadeau's career seems to be on an upswing. He finished the 2000 season at Atlanta Motor Speedway with his first Winston Cup win, becoming the first driver from Connecticut to ever win at NASCAR's highest level.

Start Me Up

Prior to Terry Labonte, NASCAR's "Iron Man" was Richard Petty. Labonte's 655 consecutive starts were a whopping 142 more than The King's 513. That's equivalent to more than three seasons worth of starts!

AP/WWP

Driver Jerry Nadeau (right) is congratulated by Gordon after winning the NAPA 500 on November 20, 2000, at Atlanta Motor Speedway.

Jack Sprague

The number 24 is usually associated with Jeff Gordon's DuPont car, but in the Craftsman Truck Series, fans of the No. 24 are cheering for Jack

David Taylor/Allsport

Jack Sprague drives his No. 24 Chevy to victory at the
Chevy Desert Classic on April 20, 1997.

Sprague. A two-time champion, Sprague is never far from the top of the pack.
The No. 24 makes Sprague a "marked man" on the track with the boo-birds
who heckle Gordon. He's said that "they booed me before they even knew
who I was just because of the number."

If you have ever attended a Craftsman truck race, you've seen Sprague in
action. That's because he's the only driver in series history to race in every
single event! Although the Craftsman Truck Series has been a launching
point for other drivers' Winston Cup careers, Sprague continues to enjoy
racing trucks. "It's great because people relate what we're driving to the
trucks they drive on the street. It's something different, something new. I
think people dig that."

Looking To The Future

Fans of the Hendrick team will have one more driver to root for in 2002.
Jimmie Johnson, currently tearing up the Busch circuit, will join the Winston
Cup Series full-time that year. The signing of young up-and-comers like
Johnson shows that Hendrick Motorsports is committed to keeping its foot off
the brake and on the accelerator in the new millennium.

Anatomy Of A Race Car

Jeff Gordon's fire-and-flames DuPont car is known as a stock car. Stock cars have several special features and modifications that allow them to race and survive speeds of 200 miles per hour.

1. **Roof flaps** – Safety feature that flips up to prevent the car from becoming airborne in a crash.

2. **Rear spoiler** – Can be adjusted to produce varying amounts of resistance.

3. **Car number** – Allows easy identification of the car in a race.

4. **Windshield** – Made of lexan, which is the same plastic used for windshields on fighter jets.

5. **Primary sponsor** – Primary sponsors have been known to pay more than $5 million to have their name and colors featured on a car.

6. **Window net** – A safety feature that prevents drivers from being thrown out of the car.

7. **Tires** – Racing tires don't have any treads to provide the driver with more traction on the road.

8. **Exhaust** – Pipes are located under the driver's side window.

9. **Arrow** – Designates where to position the jack during pit stops.

10. **Headlights** – These aren't really headlights at all. Headlights are unnecessary and a potential glass hazard, so decals are placed there instead.

11. **Grill opening** – This opening allows air to reach the radiator and brakes.

12. **Model name** – Car models currently being raced are the Chevrolet Monte Carlo, Dodge Intrepid, Ford Taurus and Pontiac Grand Prix.

13. **Engine** – Winston Cup cars use an eight-cylinder engine similar to the one found in a typical car. Unlike a regular engine, however, Winston Cup engines have been modified to have a much larger engine block that can produce significantly greater horse-power than a regular car.

14. **Fuel cell** – Located in the trunk, it serves the same purpose as a regular car's gas tank. Stock cars use a specially produced 110-octane gasoline.

15. **Taillights** – As with the headlights, stock car taillights are just decals placed over where the real taillights would go.

16. **Cooling system** – Circulates air from outside of the car onto the driver through his helmet and the holes in his seat. Keeps temperatures from becoming unbearable on hot days.

GUNNING FOR THE
CHECKERED FLAG

Career Statistics

Jeff Gordon is the among winningest racers in NASCAR history. Here's a look at how he has done throughout his NASCAR career. (Totals for 2001 are through June 10.)

Year	Starts	Wins	Top 5	Top 10	Winnings	Point Standings
1992	1	0	0	0	$6,285	#79
1993	30	0	7	11	$765,168	#14
1994	31	2	7	14	$1,607,010	#8
1995	31	7	17	23	$4,347,343	#1
1996	31	10	21	24	$2,484,518	#2
1997	32	10	22	23	$4,201,227	#1
1998	33	13	26	28	$6,175,867	#1
1999	34	7	18	21	$5,281,361	#6
2000	34	3	11	21	$2,703,590	#9
2001	14	3	9	9	$3,739,390	#1
Totals	271	55	138	174	$31,311,759	

Career Wins

Jeff Gordon amassed 50 career wins faster (and at a younger age) than any other driver in modern NASCAR history. Here's a win-by-win accounting of his checkered flags, along with some memorable race tidbits. (Totals for 2001 are through June 10.)

1994 – 2 Wins

May 29 – Coca-Cola 600, Charlotte Motor Speedway

- *This win marked Gordon's first Winston Cup victory.*

August 6 – Brickyard 400, Indianapolis Motor Speedway

- *The inaugural Brickyard 400 was also the first Winston Cup race ever held at this track, home of the famed Indianapolis 500.*

1995 –7 Wins – Winston Cup Championship

February 26 – Goodwrench 500, North Carolina Speedway

March 12 – Purolator 500, Atlanta Motor Speedway

Jeff Gordon celebrates in Victory Lane after winning the inaugural Brickyard 400 on August 6, 1994.

APWWP

Gordon toasts his Winston Cup trophy after clinching the
championship on November 12, 1995.

April 2 – Food City 500, Bristol Motor Speedway

July 1 – Pepsi 400, Daytona International Speedway

July 9 – Slick 50 300, New Hampshire International Speedway

September 3 – Mountain Dew Southern 500, Darlington Raceway

September 17 – MBNA 500, Dover Downs International Speedway

1996 – 10 Wins

March 3 – Pontiac Excitement 400, Richmond International Raceway

March 24 – TranSouth Financial 400, Darlington Raceway

March 31 – Food City 500, Bristol Motor Speedway

June 2 – Miller 500, Dover Downs International Speedway

June 16 – UAW-GM Teamwork 500, Pocono Raceway

AP/WWP

July 28 – DieHard 500, Talladega Superspeedway

September 1 – Mountain Dew Southern 500, Darlington Raceway

• *Gordon repeated history when he became only the second driver ever to win three races in a row at this track (Dale Earnhardt was the first driver to do so).*

September 15 – MBNA 400, Dover Downs International Speedway

Gordon crosses the finish line to take his first victory of the year at the Pontiac Excitement 400 on March 3, 1996.

September 22 – Hanes 500, Martinsville Speedway

- *Gordon set a record on this course on when he completed the race in 3 hours, 11 minutes and 54 seconds.*

September 29 – Tyson/Holly Farms 400, North Wilkesboro Speedway

- *This race was the last Winston Cup competition to be held at this track.*

1997 – 10 Wins –
Winston Cup Championship

February 16 – Daytona 500, Daytona International Speedway

- *This win made Gordon the youngest driver ever to win the Daytona 500.*

February 23 – Goodwrench Service 400, North Carolina Speedway

April 13 – Food City 500, Bristol Motor Speedway

April 20 – Goody's Headache Powder 500, Martinsville Speedway

May 25 – Coca-Cola 600, Charlotte Motor Speedway

Daytona 500 winner Gordon is showered with champagne by his teammates on February 16, 1997.

AP/WWP

June 8 – Pocono 500, Pocono Raceway

• *Gordon experienced tire problems early in the race that could have been devastating, but he still found a way to win.*

June 22 – California 500, California Speedway

• *On his way to victory, Gordon set a course speed record of 155.012 mph.*

August 10 – The Bud at the Glen, Watkins Glen International Speedway

• *This win marked Gordon's first on a road course. After this win, he would be nearly unstoppable on the road.*

August 31 – Mountain Dew Southern 500, Darlington Raceway

• *This win, added to wins at the Daytona 500 and the Coca-Cola 600, won Gordon the Winston Million – making him only the second NASCAR driver in the 12-year history of the event to do so (Bill Elliott was the first).*

Craig Jones/Allsport

Gordon (center) celebrates his Winston Million bonus after the Mountain Dew Southern 500 at Darlington Raceway on August 31, 1997.

AP/WWP

Gordon takes the checkered flag June 28, 1998,
at the Save Mart/Kragen 350 at Sears Point Raceway.

September 14 – CMT 300, New Hampshire International Speedway

1998 – 13 Wins –
Winston Cup Championship

February 22 – GM Goodwrench Service Plus 400, North
Carolina Speedway

March 29 – Food City 500, Bristol Motor Speedway

May 24 – Coca-Cola 600, Charlotte Motor Speedway

- *This win marked Gordon's final win at Charlotte; it changed its
  name to Lowe's Motor Speedway in 1999.*

June 28 – Save Mart/Kragen 350, Sears Point Raceway

- *Gordon's win was the first win at this newly designed racetrack.*

July 26 – Pennsylvania 500, Pocono Raceway

- *Gordon set a track record here when he led all drivers for 164 of the 200 laps.*

August 1 – Brickyard 400, Indianapolis Motor Speedway

- *This victory made Gordon the event's first two-time winner.*

August 9 – The Bud at the Glen, Watkins Glen International Speedway

August 16 – Pepsi 400, Michigan International Speedway

- *Gordon's win here was his fourth in four weeks, tying a modern-era NASCAR record.*

August 30 – CMT 300, New Hampshire International Speedway

September 6 – Pepsi Southern 500, Darlington Raceway

- *Gordon's win here marked the first time a driver had won four Southern 500 races in a row.*

AP/WWP

The newly crowned Winston Cup champion sprays champagne at a celebration after the NAPA 500 on November 8, 1998.

Gordon shakes hands with "King" Richard Petty – the man whose record for wins in a season Gordon would tie.

David Taylor/Allsport

October 17 – Pepsi 400, Daytona International Speedway

- *This race had been postponed from earlier in the year, when wild-fires threatened the racetrack.*

November 1 – AC Delco 400, North Carolina Speedway

- *This win clinched Gordon's third Winston Cup championship.*

November 8 – NAPA 500, Atlanta Motor Speedway

- *With this win, Gordon accomplished what only one other driver in modern NASCAR history had done – achieve 13 victories in one season. Who was the other driver? Richard Petty, in 1975.*

1999 – 7 Wins

February 14 – Daytona 500, Daytona International Speedway

March 14 – Cracker Barrel 500, Atlanta Motor Speedway

May 2 – California 500, California Speedway

June 27 – Save Mart/Kragen 350, Sears Point Raceway

- *This win marked Gordon's fourth consecutive road-course checkered flag.*

AP/WWP

Gordon celebrates his victory at the October 3, 1999, NAPA AutoCare 500 at Martinsville Speedway.

August 15 –
Frontier at the Glen, Watkins Glen International Speedway

• *With this win, Gordon entered the record books with five consecutive road-course wins.*

October 3 –
NAPA AutoCare 500, Martinsville Speedway

• *This was Gordon's first race without crew chief Ray Evernham.*

October 11 –
UAW-GM Quality 500, Lowe's Motor Speedway

• *Gordon set a track record here when he reached speeds of 160.306 mph on his way to victory in 3 hours, 7 minutes and 31 seconds.*

2000 – 3 Wins

April 16 – DieHard 500, Talladega Superspeedway

• *Gordon's first win after a 13-race winless streak was also his 50th career victory.*

June 25 – Save Mart/Kragen 350, Sears Point Raceway

• *With this win, his sixth consecutive road course victory, Gordon tied the record of Richard Petty, Bobby Allison and Rusty Wallace for the most career road course wins.*

September 9 – Monte Carlo 400, Richmond International Raceway

2001

March 4 – UAW-Daimler Chrysler 400, Las Vegas Motor Speedway

• *This was Gordon's first win of the 2001 season – and his first win at this track.*

June 3 – MBNA Platinum 400, Dover Downs International Speedway

• *Gordon dominated this race, leading 381 of the 400 laps for his 54th career victory.*

June 10 – Kmart 400, Michigan International Speedway

(Totals for 2001 are through June 10.)

AP/WWP

Gordon drives the final lap before taking the win at the UAW-Daimler Chrysler 400 on March 4, 2001 – his first win at Las Vegas Motor Speedway.

Career Timeline

Jeff Gordon has been racing since he was 5 years old. His career has taken him from quarter-midgets to sprint cars and, since 1993, racing stock cars full time in the NASCAR Winston Cup Series. His career inevitably has gone through some highs and lows. Here are some of the highlights.

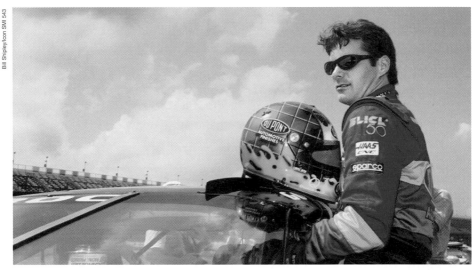

Bill Shipley/Icon SMI 543

Gordon takes in the field after a practice run at Daytona in February of 2000.

1980

Gordon's future as a champion is already beginning to come into focus when he wins 46 of 50 quarter midget races at the age of 9.

1989

Foreshadowing his future honors in the Busch Grand National and Winston Cup Series, Gordon wins the United States Auto Club Midget Rookie of the Year award.

1990

In his last full season driving midgets, Gordon wins the USAC Midget Series national championship, becoming the youngest driver ever to do so.

Gordon gets his feet wet in the stock car world, running in his first Busch Grand National race at Rockingham.

1991

Gordon becomes the USAC Silver Crown champion.

Gordon is named to the All-American Team by the American Auto Racing Writers and Broadcasters Association.

He is named Busch Grand National Series Rookie of the Year.

1992

With 11 poles, Gordon sets the Busch Grand National Series record for pole positions in a single season.

Gordon cheers after winning the Mountain Dew Southern 500 at Darlington in 1995.

APWWP

1993

Gordon bursts onto the Winston Cup scene, winning Rookie Of The Year honors.

1994

Gordon records his first Winston series victory.

Wins the Busch Clash.

1995

At the age of 24, Gordon wins the Winston Cup championship, the youngest driver ever to do so in the modern era of racing.

Wins The Winston for the first time.

Gordon is named Driver of the Year by both ESPN and the National Motorsports Press Association.

Wins over $4 million in regular season earnings, breaking the regular-season earnings record.

That's No Bull

In 1998, Gordon won the Winston No Bull 5 $1 million bonus at Darlington Raceway. With his March 2001 victory in Las Vegas, he brought his Winston No Bull 5 bonus victories to five.

APWWP

Gordon waits as his crew makes adjustments during a practice session for the 1995 NAPA 500 – the race that clinched his 1995 Winston Cup championship.

1996

Gordon is named the True Value Man of the Year.

1997

Gordon wins his second Busch Clash.

After winning the Southern 500 at Darlington, Gordon wins the Winston Million bonus, becoming only the second driver ever to do so.

Gordon leaps from the roof of his car after capturing the Winston Cup championship on Nov. 16, 1997.

APWWP

Driving his famous "Jurassic Park" car, Gordon wins The Winston a second time.

Gordon wins the 1997 Winston Cup points race.

1998

With four consecutive wins this year, Gordon tied the modern-era NASCAR record.

Wins $1.6 million at the Brickyard 400, the then-largest payday ever.

Gordon is the Winston Cup champion, and named ESPN's 1998 Driver of the Year.

Wins 13 races, tying him with Richard Petty for most wins in a season.

1999

Gordon is ranked No. 5 in a *Sports Illustrated* "Driver of the Century" poll. The pollees include some of NASCAR's most important and influential people, past and present.

Becomes the youngest driver to win the Daytona 500 twice.

Finishes the season with seven wins to become the first driver to win the most races for five years in a row.

Gordon wins seven Bud Poles, bringing his Winston Cup total to 30.

2001

Wins The Winston for the third time and ties Dale Earnhardt for the most victories in that event.

AT THE RACES

Close Calls

Stock car racing is one of the world's most thrilling – and dangerous – sports. Although he has avoided serious injury on the racetrack, Jeff Gordon has become "Crash Gordon" on more than one occasion.

August 4, 1996 – Brickyard 400 Indianapolis Motor Speedway

Sometimes a car is taken out of contention by a competitor. Sometimes engine failure is the culprit. And sometimes it's just plain rotten luck.

Gordon won the inaugural Brickyard 400 in 1994, and two years later, the hometown crowd was primed for a repeat performance by the Wonder Boy from nearby Pittsboro. Gordon's Chevy was an early contender and appeared poised to challenge throughout the race. But then, "the car was starting to handle pretty good . . . I just went in there and blew a right front [tire]. I don't know why," said Gordon. Not only did he suffer the indignity of a flat tire, but the mishap also put Gordon into the wall and into the garage for 70 laps.

The August 4 race, which fell on Gordon's birthday, was

The No. 24 DuPont skids after hitting the wall on turn 4 of the 2000 MBNA Platinum 400.

APWWP

memorable, but for all the wrong reasons. "This isn't a good birthday present," he said. "You have such high expectations going into this race and then to have a disappointing day like this makes it even more miserable."

March 28, 1999 – Primestar 500 Texas Motor Speedway

Crashes are an inevitable part of racing and drivers can avoid them only so long before the odds catch up to them. Gordon was in the worst crash of his career at the Primestar 500 at Texas Motor Speedway. It was Gordon's first 43rd-place finish of his Winston Cup career and only his second last-place finish overall.

The crash was caused when Gordon cut his right front tire and had nowhere to go but into the wall. He was lucky to escape with only a sore shoulder and some bruises. "I thought I broke ribs for sure. And luckily, it just bruised them. You don't realize how bad it is until a week and a half, two weeks later, you still can't take a full breath. And you realize that, wow, that was a heck of a hit," said Gordon.

Drivers pile up on the second lap of the 1998 Texas 500 at Texas Motor Speedway.

April 11, 1999 – Food City 500 Bristol Motor Speedway

Just two weeks after suffering the worst injuries of his career, Gordon looked to rebound at the Food City 500 at Bristol Motor Speedway. Gordon had won the previous four spring races at Bristol, and a fifth consecutive win

The Rainbow Warriors work furiously to try to fix the damage to Gordon's car after the Food City 500 collision.

would give him the modern-era record. Gordon stayed in the top 5 for most of the race and looked prepared to make a run for the checkered flag. With 160 laps remaining, Hendrick Motorsports teammate Jerry Nadeau lost control of his car, taking out leaders Tony Stewart and Gordon and sending the No. 24 car limping onto pit road. Gordon's chances at a fifth consecutive Bristol win were dashed, but he remained optimistic after finishing strong with a sixth-place finish. "This was a great comeback for our team today. The first issue was to see if I could go all the way," he said. In coming back from two crashes in two consecutive races, Gordon proved he could go all the way, and then some.

April 2, 2000 – DirecTV 500 Texas Motor Speedway

Texas Motor Speedway has long been a thorn in Gordon's side – he can't seem to win there, and he's had some memorable crashes there. At the DirecTV 500, he suffered another crushing disappointment. On lap 112, Gordon maneuvered to pass Jerry Nadeau, but collided

Bad Luck At Bristol

At the 1997 Goody's 500 at Bristol Motor Speedway, Gordon's No. 24 DuPont Chevy was walloped by Jeremy Mayfield. "That's Bristol. That's the way it goes," said Mayfield. Gordon placed the blame squarely on Mayfield. "That's what happens on a track you can't pass on," he said.

with Bill Elliott instead. Gordon could do nothing but watch as the upended Elliott rode the No. 24 Chevy's hood for several seconds. Once again, Texas Motor Speedway had gotten the better of Gordon. "It's not a place that's easy to maneuver," he said. "It's the toughest place there is to pass on the circuit. It's a one-groove race track." His pit crew did all they could to fix the battered car, even using duct tape to hold it together. Gordon's 25th-place finish was his best

effort to date at the track, where he had never finished in the top 30. It was little consolation. "I just can't seem to stay out of trouble," he lamented.

AP/WWP

Gordon and Bill Elliott collide in turn 2 on lap 112 of the 2000 DirectTV 500 at Texas Motor Speedway. Elliott would ride Gordon's hood for several hundred feet. Jerry Nadeau (No. 25) spins out in the background.

May 20, 2000 – The Winston Lowe's Motor Speedway

With no points at stake, just a lot of money, The Winston brings out the competitive spirits of the drivers. Gordon admits, "I think you'll take extra chances. You put your nose in places that maybe it doesn't belong at times." Gordon, Steve Park and Tony Stewart all got their noses into each other at the 2000 all-star race. After a series of mishaps, the crash that finally ended the race for Gordon occurred after Park was spun into an outside wall. Gordon couldn't avoid Stewart and drove

into his No. 20 car, pushing it forward into Park, and in doing so, ending any chance the three of them had at winning the Winston's huge purse.

October 8, 2000 – UAW-GM Quality 500 Lowe's Motor Speedway

Jeff Gordon had to like his chances going into the UAW-GM Quality 500. He was the reigning champion of the event, and started the 2000 race from the pole position. Unfortunately, a series of incidents sent Gordon home with a crushed front end and dashed any chance he had at victory. On lap 159, Rusty Wallace bumped Dale Jarrett, who was sent spinning into the wall. The resulting pile-up took out several drivers, including Gordon. "I hit hard enough to mess the car up, but not hard enough to hurt me. I just saw somebody spin up ahead of me, and I got on the brakes real hard . . . There was nothing but smoke, and I knew if I went to the inside I was going to get into it," said Gordon.

A crash in the fourth turn at Lowe's takes out several drivers, including Gordon.

APWWP

May 19, 2001 – The Winston
Lowe's Motor Speedway

After a first-lap crash caused by wet conditions at The Winston in 2001, Gordon's day at the races appeared to be over. But NASCAR, mindful that fans want to see their favorite drivers, allowed Gordon (and the three other drivers whose cars were damaged in the crash) to re-enter the race and use a backup car.

Gordon was back in the race, but how well would he do in a replacement car? "If we can use the backup and win this thing . . . boy, wouldn't that be a story," said Gordon before the restart.

His words proved prophetic, as he won the race and tied Dale Earnhardt for most victories at The Winston, with three. "To have a backup car that good, and to be able to pull it off the truck in that kind of situation and win The Winston, man that's just awesome," said Gordon.

AP/WWP

Gordon sits in his car after crashing in the first lap of the 2001 The Winston.
He would go on to win the non-points race in a backup car.

Race Day Experience

Watching a race on television is great, but it just doesn't compare to the experience of being trackside on race weekend. But if you're a NASCAR newcomer, there are a few things you should know before you head off to watch the action live.

Getting There Is Half The Fun

Gordon races ahead of the pack at the 2001 Carolina Dodge Dealers 400 at Darlington.

Donald Miralle/ALLSPORT

It's not a bad idea to start planning a trek out to the tracks a year ahead of time. Major races like the Daytona 500 often sell out months in advance. Tickets, which can range from being reasonably priced to amounts in the triple-digits, can be hard to obtain last-minute, but it's certainly not impossible, depending on the race and the venue. Tickets can be purchased through track box offices or on the Internet, if the track has a website.

Vantage Point

Most fans sit in the grandstands, but some tracks allow for seating in the infield – the circular green on the inside of the track. Fans usually drive their cars or motor homes onto the infield and set up camp on top of them to get a view of the track. It can be pretty hard to see all of the action from the middle, but when the grandstands are sold out, the infield is usually still available. It may be crowded, but it's the perfect spot to get to know other fans and cheer for your favorite drivers in the absolute center of the action. There's nothing like participating in a virtual block party with 43 cars screaming around the track just a few feet away!

What Do Those Flags Mean?

- Green – Signals the beginning of the race or the restart of the race after any cautions.
- Yellow – Tells drivers to maintain their positions due to dangerous conditions on the track.
- Red – Temporarily stops the race after crashes for a thorough track clean-up.
- Black – Tells a driver that he has either broken a rule or his car is a hazard to those around him and he has to pit.
- Black with White Cross – Signals that a driver's laps are no longer being counted. Second warning after black flag.
- Blue with Orange Stripe – Tells drivers who are a lap down to yield to the lead cars.
- White – Signals the beginning of the last lap.
- Checkered – Means the race is over.

Not much compares to being there – the distinctive smell of burning rubber and the roar of stock cars running full-throttle three and four wide on NASCAR's most famous tracks. Anticipation hangs in the air at any race, and

AP/WWP

Drivers take the green flag in the first 125-mile Daytona 500 qualifying race on February 11, 1999, at Daytona International Speedway.

It's great to see your favorite driver race down the stretch!

not only about who will win the race. What will Jeff Gordon's new paint scheme look like? Will Tony Stewart land in the top five? Will Dale Jr. place above Matt Kenseth? Even if you only follow one driver, you can't help but get caught up in the excitement around you – especially if you're sitting next to fans of a different driver!

NASCAR fans know that sitting in the grandstands is an intense experience. Stock car racing is touted as a family sport, so it's likely that you'll be surrounded by adults and kids of all ages, and they may all be cheering for different drivers! Just remember that it's all in good fun and that fans can sometimes be a rowdy bunch, especially if their driver isn't doing so well.

It's The Pits

Whether it's a scheduled stop or an emergency situation, watching pit stops is just as much fun as watching the race itself. And if you have a stopwatch handy, you can time the fellas in front of and behind the wall to see if they're losing time or breaking records!

Pit crews are essential to the success of a driver. Drivers hand-pick their crews and trust them to install tires correctly, diagnose (and repair!) engine problems on the spot,

What To Bring

Make sure you go to the track prepared for any situation. Here's a quick checklist of necessities:
- Binoculars
- Sunscreen
- Radio with earphones
- Raincoat/umbrella
- Earplugs
- Camera with high-powered lens
- Apparel with your driver's logo on it
- A fine-tip permanent marker and one or two items to be signed, just in case you run into your favorite driver in the garage.

and fill up the gas tank – all at the same time! They work like a well-greased engine, and watching them work is an incredible adrenaline rush.

For some drivers, the turn onto pit road may be the last turn of the race, especially if they know that there's a problem with their car. Pit crews may be experts, but sometimes it's just not safe to return to the track for more laps at a grueling 200 mph.

"Looks Like He's Outta The Race, Folks"

What happens if your driver's engine fails or if he gets disqualified during the race? You could hang around and watch the rest of the action, or you can walk around the miles of souvenir stands and team haulers in the parking lots. From shirts and hats to die-cast cars and radio scanners (to tune into specific drivers' radio frequencies), dealers and retailers are out there selling everything imaginable with your favorite driver's likeness, number or signature on it.

Jonathan Ferrey/ALLSPORT

Gordon's pit crew pushes his car with its special "NASCAR 2000" paint scheme off the track after it overheats during the 2000 Daytona 500.

And because many times drivers are easily accessible to the fans after the race, there's a good chance that you might run into your favorite NASCAR hero and he might even sign one of your new souvenirs! Walking around the grounds may also yield plenty of outstanding photo opportunities of drivers and cars that will help you remember your special day at the tracks.

Of course, when the hot sun gets the better of you and you're looking for a little peace and quiet, some tracks have recreation areas, like lakes or ponds (or beaches, like at Daytona) that can be relaxing after you've gone hoarse from cheering. And if it's shade you're looking for, try to stop by the garage to catch some behind the scenes action.

Gordon signs a cap for a fan before the final practice session of the 2001 Talladega 500.

AP/WWP

Inside Track

Being in the garage is an experience! While the press tends to hover around the drivers, so do the fans – and drivers are usually more than willing to sign autographs and share a few words with their devoted followers. Did you think that Gordon made an exceptionally exciting move on the straightaway during lap 87? Well, this is your chance to tell him! And if he had a bad day at the track, let him know that his fans still support him.

Weather Or Not

Most racetracks are located in the Southern states where racing season lasts for the majority of the year. NASCAR races are notorious for stopping and starting unexpectedly due to brief spurts of inclement weather. So, prepare to be rained on now and again! But never fear, there's plenty to see and do around the track while you're waiting for the rain delay to end and the track to dry out.

Of course, drivers spend a lot of time in the garage before the race perfecting their cars and much time after the race figuring out what went wrong, so be courteous to those working around you and watch where you're going – no one wants to run over a fan!

Since the NASCAR garage is where all the off-track action is, the average fan may not be able to get a garage pass with much ease, but they are out there, if you know the right people. Some tracks even sell them like they sell tickets, so ask around.

Whether you're sipping lemonade atop a motor home in the infield, adding to the stomping, clamoring and chanting in the grandstands or checking out the off-track action and excitement, there's no bad place to be on race day.

Inside the garage! The Rainbow Warriors work on Gordon's car before qualifying heats at Talladega in 1995.

Racetrack Review

The NASCAR Winston Cup Series visited 23 tracks over the course of 36 races in 2001. Here are the stats and the facts on each of them, including tidbits about Gordon's performances at each one.

Atlanta Motor Speedway
Hampton, Georgia

The Atlanta Motor Speedway hosts two Winston Cup races each year. Atlanta also hosts an annual Busch series race, music festivals and other civic events.

FACT: Gordon has three wins at this track to date – including his 1998 NAPA 500 win that tied him with Richard Petty's modern-era record of 13 wins in a season.

Bristol Motor Speedway
Bristol, Tennessee

Known as "The World's Fastest Half Mile," the track at Bristol hosts two Winston races per season, including one of the Winston Cup's rare night events. The half-mile track has 36-degree banking, the steepest of all NASCAR tracks.

FACT: Gordon won the Food City 500 held at this track four years in a row, from 1995 to 1998.

California Speedway
Fontana, California

The California Speedway is one of NASCAR's newest tracks. In its years of operation, the smooth two-mile, tri-oval has gained a reputation as being a favorite among drivers.

FACT: Gordon has had two first-place finishes at this speedway, and on his way to his June 22, 1997 victory, he set a course speed record of 155.012 mph.

Chicagoland Speedway
Joliet, Illinois

One of two new tracks to be added to the NASCAR circuit in 2001, Chicagoland Speedway hosted its first Winston Cup race on July 15, 2001. This 1.5-mile track is a D-shaped oval that features 11-degree banking on the front stretch and 5-degree banking on the back stretch.

FACT: Chicagoland is one of the first tracks to bring NASCAR to the Midwest.

Darlington Raceway
Darlington, South Carolina

Drivers have been racing at Darlington since 1950. Considered the "Toughest Track to Tame" because of its egg-like shape and varied turn degrees, it's hard for drivers to leave the 1.3-mile track without a "Darlington Stripe" on their cars, the traditional sign of inadvertent wall contact.

FACT: Gordon won three races in a row here – the Southern 500 in 1995 and 1996, and the TranSouth Financial 400 in 1996.

Daytona International Speedway
Daytona Beach, Florida

Home to numerous motorsports events throughout the year, Daytona International is NASCAR's most famous track. The 2.5-mile tri-oval hosts the Daytona 500, the Winston Cup's most renowned race.

FACT: The first time Gordon slid behind the wheel of a Winston Cup car was at this track in 1991, when he had the opportunity to take a spin in Mark Martin's Folgers car.

Dover Downs
International Speedway
Dover, Delaware

The "Monster Mile" is a cement oval with a lap of exactly one mile. Considered one of the most exciting tracks at which to watch a race north of the Carolinas, Dover Downs has run two Winston Cup races annually since 1971.

FACT: On September 15, 1996, Gordon claimed his third consecutive victory here, tying the records of Rusty Wallace and David Pearson.

Homestead-Miami Speedway
Miami, Florida

The inaugural Winston Cup Series race at this 1.5-mile Florida track was held in November 1999. Prior to 1999, the Homestead-Miami Speedway was used primarily for the Craftsman Truck and Busch circuit races.

FACT: In his first two Winston Cup races at this track, Gordon pulled down two top-10 victories, coming in 10th in 1999 and seventh in 2000.

Indianapolis Motor Speedway
Speedway, Indiana

Nicknamed "The Brickyard" because the track was originally brick-paved, Indianapolis became part of the Winston Cup circuit in 1994. Known best as the home of Indy car racing and the Indianapolis 500, Indianapolis' 2.5-mile rectangular track is home to NASCAR's Brickyard 400.

FACT: Gordon has driven to Victory Lane twice at the Brickyard 400, in 1994 and in 1998.

Kansas Speedway
Kansas City, Kansas

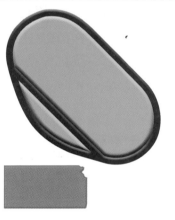

In 2001, Kansas Speedway's inaugural season, the tri-oval track set industry records for first-season ticket sales. This is due in part to the track's fan-friendly atmosphere, which provides spectacular views from every seat in the venue.

FACT: Kansas Speedway is expected to be the largest tourist attraction in the state of Kansas.

Las Vegas Motor Speedway
Las Vegas, Nevada

This tri-oval, 1.5-mile track located in the "Entertainment Capital Of The World" provides drivers with plenty of passing room, making for an enthralling race every year.

FACT: Gordon's first win of the 2001 season – and his first win at this track – took place at the UAW-Daimler Chrysler 400 on March 4, 2001. With the victory, Gordon also won the "No Bull 5" million-dollar bonus.

Lowe's Motor Speedway
Concord, North Carolina

Among the many other events held there, this North Carolina track hosts The Winston, NASCAR's all-star race, each May. Like the California Speedway, Lowe's is a favorite among drivers with its roomy 1.5-mile tri-oval track.

FACT: Gordon set a track record here on October 11, 1999, at the UAW-GM Quality 500, when he reached speeds of 160.306 m.p.h. on his way to victory in 3 hours, 7 minutes and 31 seconds.

Martinsville Speedway
Martinsville, Virginia

The smallest (0.526 miles) and oldest (1955) track on the NASCAR race schedule, Martinsville was originally a dirt track and remains the perfect place to trade paint on a Sunday afternoon.

FACT: Gordon set a record on this course on September 22, 1996, when he completed the Hanes 500 in 3 hours, 11 minutes and 54 seconds.

Michigan International Speedway
Brooklyn, Michigan

Located near Detroit, the 2-mile Michigan Speedway has one of the widest laps in NASCAR racing. It's no surprise to sometimes see three and four cars racing abreast on the D-shaped oval.

FACT: Gordon's first – and only – win here was at 1998's Pepsi 400. This victory was his fourth straight, making him only the seventh modern-era driver to attain that feat.

New Hampshire International Speedway
Loudon, New Hampshire

Loudon, the only NASCAR racetrack in New England, hosts two Winston Cup races annually. The 1.5-mile track is similar to Martinsville and offers extreme racing through 12-degree turns and 5-degree straightaways.

FACT: Gordon has had three victories at this track to date – he won the Slick 50 500 in 1995 and the CMT 300 in 1997 and 1998.

North Carolina Speedway
Rockingham, North Carolina

Otherwise known as "The Rock," this one-mile oval racetrack in North Carolina has traditionally hosted the second race of the Winston Cup season and is known for its rough surface, which inflates tire damage.

FACT: Gordon has won at The Rock four times: at the Goodwrench 500 in 1995, the Goodwrench Service 400 in 1997 and 1998 and the AC Delco 400 in 1998 (which was also the race in which he clinched his third Winston Cup championship).

Phoenix International Raceway
Phoenix, Arizona

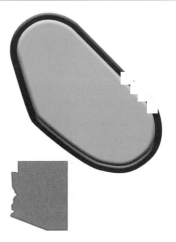

This D-shaped, one-mile desert track is known for its complex turns and majestic surroundings. Since 1964, the raceway has been host to all divisions of racing.

FACT: Of all the Winston Cup tracks that Gordon has raced in his career, this is one of two where he has yet to win (Texas is the other). In his best outing here, he finished fourth in the Slick 50 500 in 1994.

Pocono Raceway
Long Pond, Pennsylvania

Pocono Raceway is a superspeedway and road course all in one package. When preparing for a race at Pocono, drivers must build their cars to conquer tight turns and thrilling straightaways on the 2.5-mile triangle.

FACT: Gordon set a track record here on July 26, 1998, when he led all drivers for 164 of the 200 laps at the Pennsylvania 500 on his way to the checkered flag.

Richmond International Raceway
Richmond, Virginia

Racers and fans have frequented Richmond since its dirt-track days in the 1940s. Redesigned to accommodate today's stock cars, the three-quarter-mile track is an enjoyable site for fans and drivers alike.

FACT: On May 13, 1999, Gordon set a Winston Cup qualifying round record at this track when he reached a speed of 126.499 mph.

Sears Point Raceway
Sonoma, California

Sears Point, one of two road courses on the Winston Cup circuit, is marked by hills and valleys unique to the Sonoma Valley. The 11-turn course is almost two miles long and hosts one race annually.

FACT: To date, Gordon has had three straight victories at the Dodge/Save Mart 350 here, in 1998, 1999 and 2000, and since 1995, has never finished lower than sixth at this racetrack.

Talladega Superspeedway
Talladega, Alabama

Talladega is considered to be the fastest racetrack on the NASCAR circuit. Racers have set world speed records on this Alabama racetrack that stretches just more than 2.5 miles in length.

FACT: Gordon has won at this racetrack twice, at the DieHard 500 in 1996 and 2000.

Texas Motor Speedway
Fort Worth, Texas

The second-largest sports arena in the country, this quad-oval speedway runs 1.5 miles with 24-degree banking in the turns. With its resort-like amenities, fans flock here every year.

FACT: This is the second of the two tracks that Gordon can't seem to tackle – but, things are looking up! Previously, he had finished no better than 25th. In 2001, he finished fifth!

Watkins Glen
International Speedway
Watkins Glen, New York

Known for its unusual right-hand turns, this track has been host to many road-racing series. NASCAR held its first race here in 1957.

FACT: Gordon won the checkered flag at the Glen three years in a row, at the Bud at the Glen in 1997 and 1998, and the Frontier at the Glen in 1999.

Gordon's Favorite Tracks

With more than 50 wins in 10 Winston Cup seasons, Jeff Gordon has succeeded on short tracks, superspeedways and road courses. Here are eight tracks that Gordon particularly enjoys.

Atlanta Motor Speedway

Atlanta Motor Speedway wasn't always one of Gordon's favorite tracks. Prior to his back-to-back wins here in 1998 and 1999, Gordon finished out of the top 30 (and once out of the top 40!) on more than one occasion. Fortunately, those poor efforts are a thing of the past. "Atlanta has turned into a track that I'm actually looking forward to coming to," Gordon has said.

Atlanta Motor Speedway has become one of Gordon's top tracks.

M. David Leeds/Allsport

In addition to his three Winston Cup wins at Atlanta, Gordon also earned his first Busch Series win here back in 1992. "It was my first NASCAR win and I won from the pole. That was also the race that Rick Hendrick was watching that prompted him to talk to me about racing Winston Cup with Hendrick Motorsports," remembered Gordon.

Bristol Motor Speedway

Described as "The World's Fastest Half Mile," Tennessee's Bristol Motor Speedway quickly became one of Gordon's favorites. "It's just one of those

race tracks that I took to right away," said Gordon in an interview. "It reminds me of some of the tracks I used to race with the sprint cars and midgets. It's really fast and high-banked. We've had good success and I always look forward to going back to Bristol. I know the fans certainly enjoy it, too. There's no more spectacular place to race than at Bristol. It's pretty awesome."

And Gordon's four consecutive wins at Bristol Motor Speedway's Food City 500 from 1995 to 1998 are pretty awesome, too.

Gordon loves racing on "the world's fastest half mile."

Darlington Raceway

"The Track Too Tough To Tame?" Tell that to Jeff Gordon – he apparently hasn't heard that phrase applied to this South Carolina track. He has won five races here, including four consecutive Southern 500s from 1995 to 1998. "Any time you win at Darlington, it's special," said Gordon. "For drivers and teams that win here, it carries a lot of respect among your peers. That probably means as much as anything."

Daytona International Speedway

The Daytona 500, known as "The World's Greatest Race," is also the kickoff to the Winston Cup season. In 1997, at the age of 26, Gordon became the youngest driver ever to win the Daytona 500. Gordon's win was surprising to many, because some drivers race their entire career without a win in the Daytona 500 – it took even the great Dale Earnhardt 20 years to do it!

Gordon repeated his triumph in 1999. "After coming off the amazing season we had in '98, winning the first and most prestigious race of the year was just awesome. It's an honor to be added to the list of multiple Daytona 500 winners," said Gordon.

It's a celebration in Victory Lane after Gordon wins the 1999 Daytona 500.

Daytona International Speedway is also home to the Pepsi 400, traditionally held 4th of July weekend. Unlike some racetracks, at which Gordon is successful at one race, but not another, he has no such problems at Daytona, where he is also a multiple winner of the Pepsi 400.

Indianapolis Motor Speedway

When Indianapolis Motor Speedway let stock cars race across its fabled track in 1994, Jeff Gordon was given the opportunity to put on a winning performance for the hometown Indiana crowd. He didn't disappoint. "One of my favorite races each year is the Brickyard 400 at the Indianapolis Motor Speedway. I like that particular race because I grew up just outside of Indianapolis. I was able to win the inaugural Brickyard 400, and I always dreamed of racing on that track while I was growing up," said Gordon.

In 1998, Gordon made history again when he became the first repeat champion of the Brickyard 400. "To go back to my hometown, and be the first to win two Brickyard 400s at a place like Indianapolis Motor Speedway . . . was just overwhelming," he enthused.

AP/WWP

Gordon holds up his trophy after winning the inaugural Brickyard 400 on August 6, 1994.

Michigan International Speedway

Jeff Gordon won an amazing 27 races over the course of the 1995, 1996 and 1997 Winston Cup seasons, but incredibly, none of those wins came at Michigan International Speedway in Brooklyn. That changed in 1998, when Gordon recorded his first win at the racetrack.

Even before the win became reality, Gordon had enjoyed racing at Michigan. When asked once what his favorite track was, Gordon replied, "I get asked this so much, I think that we race on so many tracks and each one has different things about it that I love and things I dislike. But for an all-around track, I'll pick Michigan. It's so wide, and there is always room to pass. At this last race at Michigan, I didn't know why it was my favorite because I hadn't won there, but now

Sunglasses At Night

In 1998, Gordon's Pepsi 400 victory occurred during the first-ever "under the lights" race at Daytona.

that I have, [it] is especially one of my favorites." Some of Michigan's appeal comes from its layout. "I like the faster tracks, with two or three different grooves. Michigan is my favorite," said Gordon.

Richmond International Raceway

When Gordon was asked what kind of racetrack he would design if given the opportunity, he admitted his track would be similar to Virginia's Richmond International Raceway. "I like Richmond . . . The shape of Richmond lets us put on a great race," said Gordon. Richmond hosts two Winston Cup events each year, the Pontiac Excitement 400 and the Chevrolet Monte Carlo 400, and Gordon has won them both. If he ever decides to build the track of his dreams, Gordon's opponents are likely to be left with nothing but nightmares.

Gordon has said the shape of Richmond's track allows the drivers to put on a great race, as they do here at the 2000 Chevrolet 400.

Watkins Glen International

Road courses require a special combination of speed and skill. Watkins Glen, in New York, is no exception, with several tricky turns over the course of its grueling 2.45 miles. "I especially like racing on road course tracks such as Watkins Glen, because they present such a challenge to me," said Gordon, who won at the Glen in 1997, 1998 and 1999.

Success on road courses didn't come overnight for the DuPont-sponsored driver. "I remember the first time I started running on road courses, how lost I was. I didn't know if I would ever get it," said Gordon. It took only a few years for him to succeed beyond his wildest dreams. Gordon's unstoppable success on road courses has left competitors scratching their heads at how to beat him. Sterling Marlin offered a humorous solution, joking, "Actually, I do have the sure-fire way of somebody else winning on these road courses. All the drivers are going to get together, take up a collection, and sponsor Jeff in Formula One for a year." Unfortunately for Marlin and the other drivers, Gordon is sticking to stock cars for the foreseeable future.

APWWP

The chief starter waves the checkered flag as Gordon takes the win at the 1999 Frontier at the Glen. Gordon has quite a record at Watkins Glen, where this race was held.

Life Behind The Wheel

Stock car racing is an endurance sport and a game of strategy all wrapped up into one exciting package. Let's take a look at what a typical day behind the wheel can be like for Jeff Gordon.

It can get mighty hot in that car – up to 140°! Drivers need plenty of fluids.

To compete in NASCAR, drivers must be up for the challenge of driving 500 miles around the same track for hours – and they're not going for the traditional Sunday drive, either! With speeds that can be clocked at more than 200 mph and the heat cranked up to blistering in the cockpit, there's no room for error, fatigue or even the slightest bit of hesitation.

Suiting Up

Drivers have to be mentally prepared for race day, and the comfort of a regular routine goes a long way in easing the pre-race jitters. While Gordon's team is hard at work making last-minute adjustments to his car following the practice run, he suits up in his fireproof uniform, full-face helmet, driving gloves and specialized shoes. Inside the car, Gordon's wife, Brooke, has

Hot Enough For You?

On a hot day at a track like Alabama's Talladega, the temperature in Gordon's car can get up to 140° F. Worse, the passenger side window of the car is closed off, so hot air can't escape from that side.

taped a Scripture verse from the Bible to the steering wheel to comfort and inspire him through the long race to come.

Getting In And Starting The Engine

He's suited up, the car is all set and the race is about to begin. Gordon is ready to get into the driver's seat, but he can't just open the door, because the car doesn't have any door handles. Actually, it doesn't even have any doors! Drivers must be agile enough to slip in through the window, because that's the only way to get in!

As he slides into the driver's seat, Gordon will notice that it is perfectly formed to his body. In order to prevent neck and back injuries, seats are cast to the driver's frame to ensure that there's no room for jostling about at the wheel. If Gordon finds himself spinning on the track, the shape of his seat will help keep him in place so he'll be better able to steer himself to safety. Recently, Gordon has begun wearing the HANS (head and neck support) device, which provides more security in case of a crash.

Let's Get Ready To Race!

For the longer-endurance races on the circuit, a driver must be able to pace himself or herself. Sure, the car is a rumbling powerhouse, but it's also a delicate machine that, when run too hard and for too long, could very easily stop performing.

In The Blink Of An Eye

Sometimes trouble happens too quickly for even the spotter to react. After the 19-car pileup in the 2001 Daytona 500, Gordon was asked if his spotter had had time to warn him. Gordon replied, "My spotter didn't have time to hit the button on his radio."

Doin' it "Dukes Of Hazzard" style – drivers have to slide in through the window.

APNWWP

Tires are also key to a driver's performance on the racetrack. They're filled and treated differently depending on the characteristics of each and every racetrack. A blown tire can, at the very least, take

On Your Mark, Get Set . . .

To get ready for a race, Gordon drinks lots of fluids the night before and day of the race. He also does some pre-race stretching so that he won't cramp up in the race car.

Gordon down a few laps, and at the most, cause a run-in with another driver, a spinout or a bump against the wall. Any of these incidents can destroy the aerodynamics of Gordon's car or, if it's severe enough, even take him out of the race entirely.

What a headache! Gordon cut a tire during the final practice for the 2000 Winston 500 at Talladega and had to go to a backup car.

The number of tires Gordon and his team use depends on the particular racetrack and the length of the race. The harder a track is, the faster the tires will wear down. On softer tracks like Daytona, Gordon may have to pit for gas before his tires even need to be changed. But even though he may not need new tires yet, his crew may change them just to enable Gordon to make fewer pit stops.

See The Spotter Run

Stock cars also do not have any mirrors, so drivers can't see behind them, but even if they could, their helmet and neck supports make their side vision almost useless. So now what? How can Gordon pass his competitors without knowing who's around him? Now would be a good time for him to turn on his headset.

Throughout the race, Gordon and his fellow drivers are in direct radio contact with a teammate called a spotter. He (or she) is perched on top of the team's trailer in the infield and his job is to watch every piece of action on the track. He'll maintain continuous contact with Gordon, keeping him aware of his competitors and who's behind and next to him on the track. He'll also suggest strategies to help Gordon overtake his opponents.

AP/WWP

Spotters are aware of everything going on on the track and communicate important strategies to their drivers, like telling Gordon when to pass Dale Jarrett.

Spotters also keep an eye out for any wear to the tires or car. They know how much a tire can take, and they communicate constantly with their drivers. They work together to develop strategies for pit stops, including when it's the best time for a driver to come down pit road and how much service the car should get. If Gordon thinks his tires are holding up fine, and he's not feeling any reluctance in his brakes, but his fuel is running low, he may tell his spotter that he'll be coming in for a "gas and go." Gordon will also communicate with his crew chief throughout the race. The chief may advise patience when Gordon is getting frustrated, while Gordon will keep him informed on the condition of the track and the car.

Taste The Victory

Now the race is well under way and nearing the final laps, but Gordon finds himself running in third place during the last two laps. It's time for some strategizing.

With his hands hot on the steering wheel, he feels secure that he can pass the second-place car on the next turn. He's been running high on the turns all afternoon and if Gordon's spotter says "Clear low!," Gordon will sneak past the other driver on the low side of the track the second he gets close enough.

Gordon completes the move successfully, and with second place secured, everyone is cheering him on to the finish. The race leader is probably sweating, knowing that Gordon is so close and is actively eyeing his position.

Gordon might sneak up close to the leader and accelerate until they're both side by side. He'll wedge himself close so that the other driver is forced to the high side of the track, slowing his momentum.

Mission accomplished! Gordon has nudged the leader out of the way and the checkered flag belongs to him! Now he's running his victory lap! The fans are cheering and he knows Brooke and his teammates are waiting for him in Victory Lane!

David Taylor/Allsport

Jeff Gordon and Mike Skinner are neck and neck – who will get to taste sweet victory?

Victory has never been sweeter as Gordon climbs on top of his car! The crew will bang out those dents later, but right now, with flashes going off and microphones thrust in his face, Gordon has got his crew to thank and sponsors to please. He gives that champagne (or Pepsi) bottle a shake and celebrates!

AP/WWP

RIVALS
OF THE ROAD

The Classic Rival

On the racetrack, they were fierce competitors. Off the racetrack, they had nothing but respect and admiration for each other. The respective fans of Jeff Gordon and the late Dale Earnhardt, however, never had regard for the other driver and booed him every chance they could.

When it came to Dale Earnhardt, Gordon always listened with an open ear.

While Jeff Gordon was holding steady in the 1997 Daytona 500, the legendary Dale Earnhardt was a place ahead of him. It seemed almost guaranteed that the Man In Black might be just several laps away from taking the checkered flag at Daytona for the first time in his illustrious 20-year career.

But, as Gordon came up next to Earnhardt to take the lead, it became clear that this would be Gordon's chance for a first-time Daytona win instead. Especially when Earnhardt's car spun out of control and rammed into the wall. In the process, Earnhardt's tire left a skid mark on the side of Gordon's multicolored Chevy, truthfully an accident. But, to Earnhardt's fans, that skid was a mark of shame against Gordon, yet another reason for them to despise Daytona's youngest victor. To them, Gordon had cheated their hero out of another shot at the Super Bowl of NASCAR, and they would never let him forget it.

An Unlikely Conflict

At first, the conflict between the two drivers doesn't seem to make any sense. Both Earnhardt and Gordon were incredible drivers, adept at zooming

A familiar scene – Gordon and Earnhardt racing neck and neck.
Here they are in action during a practice round for the 1999 Las Vegas 400.

into victory lane and filling their shelves with Winston Cups. They both showed the world what a Chevrolet Monte Carlo could do on a racetrack with a determined driver at the wheel. Both men inspired legions of devoted fans who followed them everywhere, cheering all the way. And both Gordon and Earnhardt were mega-celebrities, capable of drawing huge crowds anywhere they went.

But throughout Gordon's early NASCAR career, his bright rainbow and Earnhardt's black never quite mixed, at least not according to the drivers' respective fans. At every NASCAR race, you could count on Gordon's fans jeering their lungs out when the Intimidator took center stage, and on Earnhardt loyalists booing the arrival of Gordon with a vengeance. And the last thing you wanted to do was cheer too loudly for Gordon when you were surrounded by people with the number 3 on their shirts.

In a sport where drivers battle it out on the pavement and sometimes almost come to blows in pit road after trading a little paint, it's rather

Take That!

After winning the 1995 Brickyard 400, Earnhardt joked about Gordon's age. Since Gordon had won the inaugural race the previous year, Earnhardt joked that he was the first "man" to win it.

surprising to realize that the Wonder Boy and the Man In Black rarely showed a rivalry off the track. Earnhardt was famed for battling the likes of Darrell Waltrip and Rusty Wallace over a few crashing incidents, going so far as to flip Jeremy Mayfield the finger after Mayfield passed him at the 2000 Pocono 500 ("I was telling him he was number one," joked Earnhardt later). But nothing like that ever happened between Earnhardt and Gordon. So why were the fans so rabid about each other's drivers when the drivers themselves weren't?

Stealing Thunder

In his long career, Earnhardt's record was one to be envied. During his time on the track, he put together more than 20 years of excellent finishes, seven Winston Cups and some of the most entertaining driving since Richard Petty ruled the track in his 35-year career. Even Earnhardt's solitary Daytona 500 victory in 1998 (a season in which he won no other race) was cause for joy among his fans.

Gordon races past Earnhardt to take the checkered flag at the 1999 Daytona 500 – something Earnhardt's legions of fans didn't like one bit.

Suddenly, along came this upstart outsider from Indiana (or California, depending on whom you asked), barely out of his rookie year, who won his first Winston Cup in 1995 at the age of 24. Three years later, Gordon won a third championship – at an age at which Earnhardt was just getting started in his racing career.

When Gordon won his 50th victory in 2000, Earnhardt fans were amazed at the Wonder Boy's success in such a short time. They were painfully aware that Earnhardt hadn't taken home a Winston Cup since 1994. It wasn't long before some of Earnhardt's traditional fans discarded their Intimidator T-shirts and No. 3 hats and started buying up rainbow-themed Gordon gear and cheering for NASCAR's new favorite son.

The New Blood

Many of the NASCAR fans who jumped on the Gordon bandwagon were the offspring of Earnhardt fans. This new generation loved and respected

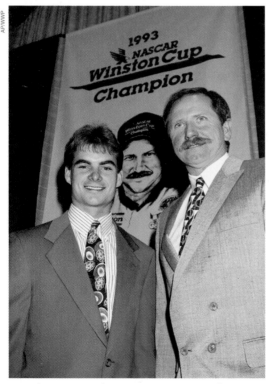

NASCAR just like their parents and grandparents, but they needed a new hero, and Gordon was the driver to fit the bill. They readily embraced the good-looking, upright young man who was so different from the gruff and chiseled "good old boys" who had populated NASCAR for so long.

Earnhardt's die-hard fans didn't like that one bit. Their hero, the man who had raised the standards of NASCAR and inspired every driver to improve in the hopes of beating him, was being upstaged by someone who was unlike any other driver NASCAR had ever seen.

Gordon poses with 1993 Winston Cup champion Earnhardt during a New York press conference.

To many Earnhardt fans, Gordon had taken a sport that

originated in the rural back roads of the South and polished it into a live-action video game – the MTV version of stock-car racing. Rather than a Southern boy with blue-collar roots, NASCAR's rising star was now a young man from the Midwest who rarely got engine oil on his hands and had looks worthy of a *GQ* cover model. To Earnhardt's die-hard corps of supporters, the Wonder Boy was nothing but a sad reminder of how much their favorite sport had changed in the image-conscious, media-friendly NASCAR of the 1990s.

And many of Gordon's fans saw the Intimidator as a washed-up redneck driver whose brightest days were behind him, someone would should let the younger and hipper generation pass him by on their way to Victory Lane. This mindset was fairly typical of how NASCAR was changing at the dawn of a new millennium, with one foot in the old days, the other in a shiny future of neon colors and celebrity drivers. As the fans berated each other's heroes, it became obvious just how different both drivers were.

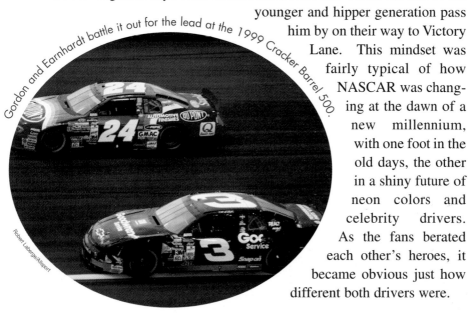

Gordon and Earnhardt battle it out for the lead at the 1999 Cracker Barrel 500.

Robert Laberge/Allsport

Different Roads

Earnhardt was a veteran driver from a respected stock-car family. Born in rural North Carolina, he had learned the art of driving from his father, Ralph, who was an accomplished driver on the NASCAR Sportsman Division circuit in the 1950s.

After dropping out of high school to race full time, Dale Earnhardt supported himself through menial jobs, and built up a mountain of bank debts on the way to his 1975 NASCAR debut. The road to success for the Intimidator was a long and hard one, filled with hardships and the failure of two marriages. It was after nearly a decade of hard work and little appreciation until Earnhardt became a full-time NASCAR driver in 1979.

Although Gordon and Earnhardt had both become fascinated by racing at a tender age, their paths were still profoundly different. Gordon had been racing since the age of 5. He had sharpened his skills on the quarter midget circuit and moved on to sprint cars, earning a license to race before he had one to drive on the highway. He showed off his amazing driving prowess at Buck Baker's racing school instead of struggling as a fill-in driver, as Earnhardt had done. By the time Gordon made it to the Winston Cup Series in 1993, he had already been driving professionally for almost 20 years.

The reaction of many fans to a driver like this, someone who had come into the world of racing in such a non-traditional way, was devastating. Gordon was savagely booed at numerous tracks, vilified by fans of old-school drivers like Earnhardt. Fictional rumors that he and his pit crew cheated NASCAR regulations abounded for years, and prompted many traditionalists to hate the Wonder Boy more than ever.

Image Overhaul

The public image of NASCAR was something else that divided Earnhardt's and Gordon's fans. For generations, stock-car racing had been

Gordon (No. 24) and Tony Stewart (No. 20) have helped to usher in a new era of Winston Cup racing — something not all of Earnhardt's fans appreciate.

AP/WWP

Gordon wears a No. 3 cap in honor of the late NASCAR champion at the Dura Lube 400 on February 25, 2001 – one week after Earnhardt's tragic death.

seen by the public as a pastime for Southerners. And, for many lifelong fans of NASCAR, Dale Earnhardt was the embodiment of everything for which the sport stood. He was a country boy who made good, someone who had risen to the highest position of NASCAR fame, yet lived his entire life in his home state of North Carolina and still went hunting and fishing with the buddies he had known since childhood. Even though he owned a huge farm in North Carolina, Earnhardt still did much of the farm work himself. While he gave the occasional interview, you could tell that Earnhardt was much more at home behind the wheel of his Chevy than in front of a camera.

But Gordon was a different story. With his boyish good looks and media-savvy personality, he was a marketer's dream in ways that Earnhardt never was. His clean-cut image came along at just the right time, a time when NASCAR was seeking to break out of its traditional image and reinvent itself as a young and dynamic sport for the new millennium. It wasn't until Gordon came along that a NASCAR driver could have hoped to be voted as one of *PEOPLE* magazine's 50 most beautiful people.

In the days of Earnhardt's ascendency, drivers were just drivers, not models or advertising tools. Gordon's boy-next-door image changed all that, paving the way for

Who's "King Of The Hill"?

A 1998 episode of the Fox animated series "King Of The Hill" played up the Earnhardt-Gordon rivalry. Earnhardt lent his voice to the episode, but Gordon declined. Of his decision Gordon said, "I was supposed to rip Earnhardt, but I wasn't interested in doing it. I guess Dale didn't mind, though," he added with a grin.

a new world of advertising for NASCAR drivers. No one ever expected the tough-as-nails Earnhardt to be involved with anything except hard-core driving. But, before long, there he was on the Wheaties box. It was hard for many of Earnhardt's fans to associate their favorite paint-trading driver with something like cereal. But that was the new era of NASCAR ushered in by Gordon.

Earnhardt On Gordon

"He's young, he's, you know, grass-root, he's good for the sponsors, he's good for NASCAR. I'd just like to beat him more often."

Two Old Soldiers

Earnhardt and Gordon never let the rivalry between their fans get in the way of their mutual respect for each other.

The vastly different Earnhardt and Gordon rarely spent time together off the track, since their non-driving interests were so different. It would have been hard to imagine Earnhardt mastering a video game, or Gordon hefting a hunting rifle.

But the fan rivalry still mystified the two drivers themselves. No matter how much paint the two of them traded, how many crashes they were involved in, how many losses they suffered to the other or how many differences they had between them, Earnhardt and Gordon both maintained an honest and healthy respect for each other.

Earnhardt could never understand why his fans blamed Gordon for the 1997 wreck at Daytona, and always made it clear that the crash hadn't been Gordon's fault – it was just bad luck. Earnhardt assured his fans that his time to pull down the checkered flag at Daytona would come.

To Earnhardt, Gordon wasn't a laughable character to be booed at the track. He was just another worthy opponent, a competitor to beat. Earnhardt recognized Gordon's incredible skills and talents behind the wheel, and never let the fan rivalry get in the way of that.

Gordon was the same way. Earnhardt was a driver to whom he often looked for advice, and got it. the Wonder Boy knew there was much to be learned from the Man In Black, and Earnhardt probably learned a few things from Gordon – even if their fans thought differently.

One final battle – Earnhardt and Gordon at the 2001 Daytona 500.

In addition to their mutual respect as drivers, Gordon and Earnhardt also had mutual business interests. When he was alive, Earnhardt was an active shareholder in Action Performance Companies, Inc., the company that produces the die-cast cars bought by millions of fans on both sides of the Gordon-Earnhardt issue. Gordon was an active shareholder then as well, and

The Classic Rival

continues to be today. No matter what their differences on the track may have been, they both knew how to turn their careers into lucrative investments.

When Dale Earnhardt tragically lost his life at the 2001 Daytona 500, Gordon was as shaken as anyone by the loss of NASCAR's greatest legend. "Not only is it a huge loss for this sport, but a huge loss for me personally," said Gordon's press release following the accident. "Dale taught me so much and became a great friend."

Gordon drives past the No. 3 sign honoring Earnhardt
at the March 24, 2001, Food City 500.

Now that the Intimidator is gone, it's hard to imagine Jeff Gordon without such an intense fan rivalry. But he'll always be able to get by on his own merits. After all, Gordon is sure to be the driver who takes NASCAR into the 21st century – and far, far, beyond.

Budding Rivals

When you race the same competitors upward of 30 times in any given year, rivalries are bound to spring up. In his 10-year Winston Cup career, Jeff Gordon has traded paint with the best of them. Here are some of the drivers who make sparks fly on the racetrack whenever they go head-to-head with Gordon.

Tony Stewart

Perhaps no other competitor on the Winston Cup circuit can get Jeff Gordon as fired up as Tony Stewart can. The two, who were born within a few months of each other, are similar in many ways. Both came to Winston Cup racing by way of open-wheel midgets and sprint cars, and their rivalry can be traced back to those early days.

Stewart, the 1999 Winston Cup Rookie of the Year, is a hard-charging driver who is not afraid to express his feelings on or off the track, and his desire for victory equals that of Gordon. Neither Gordon nor Stewart likes to give an inch on the track, and perhaps this has led to some of their more memorable confrontations.

Gordon smiles as Tony Stewart holds a finger over his head at a 1999 press conference.

One of their most heated moments came on August 13, 2000, at Watkins Glen. On the race's second lap, Gordon pulled alongside Stewart in a place where there wasn't room to pass. Somebody had to give way, but no one did, and it was Gordon who paid the price. He was forced into the wall, damaging both his car and Stewart's along the way. Gordon lost a lap as his pit crew worked feverishly to repair the No. 24 DuPont.

This race had personal significance to Gordon. Had he won it, he would have added to his string of consecutive road course wins, bringing the total to seven. No one can say what the outcome of the race had been if Gordon and Stewart hadn't clashed, but the damage to Gordon's car was severe enough for his hopes to be dashed.

Maybe Gordon's frustration over seeing his streak snapped was partially to blame for the shouting match that erupted between Stewart and Gordon after the race. The two drivers parked in the garage area, and as they were getting out of their cars, Stewart yelled, "You'd better practice what you preach. You're always telling me to take it easy on the first lap." Gordon replied, "I'll slam you into the wall the first chance I get. I'll run you straight into the wall the next time you're anywhere near me. I owe you one now buddy." Stewart, never being one to back down, shouted back, "Come over here and we'll talk about it." Fortunately, some of Stewart's crew stepped in and restrained the two before any "talking" could be done. (Coincidentally,

Stewart passes Gordon on his way to his first Winston Cup victory during the 1999 Exide 400 at Richmond International Raceway.

Stewart (No. 20) spins Gordon (No. 24) on pit road after the 2001 Food City 500 at Bristol Motor Speedway. Stewart was fined $10,000 for the incident.

Stewart and Gordon crashed into each other at the very next race, but both called it an accident.)

Both Stewart and Gordon have tried to downplay any talk of rivalry, with Gordon saying, "If there is a so-called competitive rivalry out here I guess we're it. But every car is my rival when I'm racing . . . Just seems like Tony and I are developing a little history."

Stewart Lends A Helping Hand

After Tony Stewart was fined $10,000 for the pit road incident, money started arriving at his race shop to help him pay the fine. In response, Stewart posted a letter to his fans on his website promising to match all the money he received and donate it to the Make-A-Wish Foundation. Incidentally, Make-A-Wish is one of Gordon's favorite charities.

It's clear, however, that these two talented drivers can get under each other's skin. Take, for instance, the March 25, 2001, incident at the Food City 500 at Bristol Motor Speedway. Gordon made contact with Stewart on the last lap, causing Stewart to spin out and go from fourth to 25th place, while Gordon ended up in fourth instead. In retaliation, Stewart drove onto pit road during the cool-down lap and purposely hit Gordon's car, sending it spinning into the wall that separates the pit area from the track.

Both drivers, along with their crew chiefs and owners, were hauled into the NASCAR trailer after the pit road incident, and Stewart was fined $10,000 for the offense and placed on probation.

These are clearly two competitors who don't like to lose – especially to each other. Stewart and Gordon both have many years of Winston Cup racing ahead of them, which means more fiery displays of rivalry to entertain fans for a long time to come.

Jeff Burton

After Gordon's dramatic victory over Burton at the 1997 Southern 500, he said, "I ran him [Burton] real hard. All of these people came here today to see a heck of a show, and I think they saw one."

The two Jeffs – Gordon and Burton – have found themselves neck and neck in many a Winston Cup race, but mostly without the heated displays that characterize many of the Gordon/Stewart meetings. Still, Gordon said in 1999 of Burton, "We're both young, and both of us hate to get beat by anybody. You have to be excited about this kind of thing." For his part, Burton said, "If, at the end of our careers, they talk about Jeff and I like some of the other great rivalries in NASCAR's history, then that would be an honor."

Back in 1997, it seemed likely that Burton and Gordon would indeed be great rivals (Tony Stewart hadn't entered Winston Cup racing yet). Burton and Gordon were racing in the Southern 500 at Darlington Raceway, and the Winston Million bonus was on the line for Gordon. They were running side by side on the last lap, and the two cars bumped, with Gordon finally pulling ahead to win by a car length.

Jamie Squire/Allsport

Gordon and Burton battle it out at the 1999 Goody's Body Pain 500 at Martinsville Speedway.

After the race, Burton said, "I wasn't racing for the million dollars. I was racing to win the Southern 500. The million dollars didn't mean a thing to me other than if he couldn't win it, I wanted to be the one who kept him from doing it."

Burton was criticized for not being agressive enough on the track to keep Gordon from winning. Perhaps if Burton had bumped Gordon a little harder, some said, he could have pushed Gordon out of the way and given himself the victory. No way, replied Burton. The racetrack is a dangerous place as it is, and he did not want to deliberately cause an accident.

Burton and Gordon keep their rivalry on the racetrack. "I like Jeff Gordon," Burton said. "Jeff Gordon's a nice guy, and he's done a lot for the sport."

They clashed again in 1998 at Richmond, when Gordon whittled down Burton's lead until the two were racing side by side to the finish, with Burton finishing 0.051 seconds ahead of Gordon. Some felt that Gordon allowed the Burton the win, since Burton had been courteous to Gordon the previous year. Burton seemed to agree, saying, "I've always driven Jeff clean, and he drove me clean tonight, I feel what I gave last year came back to me tonight. Had we wrecked last year at Darlington," he said, "I bet this outcome would have been different."

Dale Jarrett

Dale Jarrett and Jeff Gordon were neck and neck for the Winston Cup title midway through the 2001 season, but this isn't the first time the two have raced each other with high stakes on the line. In 1999, during the Jiffy Lube 300 at New Hampshire International Speedway, Gordon bumped his way past Winston Cup points-leader Jarrett into a third-place finish.

Dale Jarrett leads Gordon during the 2000 Pop Secret Microwave Popcorn 400. Jarrett would go on to win.

After the race, Jarrett and Gordon

Always A Bridesmaid?

In 2000, Dale Jarrett took the checkered flag in the Pop Secret Microwave Popcorn 400 at Rockingham, beating Gordon by 2.197 seconds after finishing second several times at the track. A relieved Jarrett said, "Finally. No more bridesmaid here."

began a bit of a yelling match. After the incident, Jarrett was quoted as saying, "[Gordon] hit me once down Turns 1 and 2, and then I blocked him down the backstretch. Then he ran in the back of me, not once, but three times in Turns 3 and 4. We have a lot of racing to do. We'll see each other again."

Gordon had a different take on the situation. He replied, "There's nobody I want to race any cleaner than D.J., but I think the heat of the moment kind of got to both of us. We'll patch things up. Me and D.J. are fine."

As the 2001 Winston Cup points race gets tighter, watch for the sparks to keep flying between Gordon and Jarrett.

Gordon and Dale Jarret (right) lead the pack to the green flag at the start of the Cracker Barrel 500 at Atlanta Motor Speedway March 11, 2001.

Rusty Wallace

Veteran driver Rusty Wallace and Gordon have done their share of "bumpin' and scrapin'" over the years. After an incident at Richmond International Raceway in 1998 in which Wallace spun Gordon into a wall and out of contention, NASCAR observers wondered if it was payback for

Gordon knocking Wallace out of the lead 14 months previous at Bristol Motor Speedway. Clearly, these two men have a history.

In 1999, Gordon and Wallace raced to see who would be the first to attain 50 career Winston Cup victories, with Wallace acknowledging, "I'd like to get my 50th before he does." Ultimately, Wallace did get to the magic number before Gordon.

Gordon attempts to pass Rusty Wallace on his way to eventual victory at the June 3, 2001, MBNA Platinum 400 at Dover Downs.

Their rivalry has continued into 2001. After Wallace ran Gordon up the banking in the final laps of the Pontiac Excitement 400 at Richmond in May, allowing Tony Stewart to get the win, Gordon bumped Wallace in the cool-down lap.

Taking It To A New Level

Of racing Gordon, Wallace once said, "I think it's good for everybody to compete to a new level. Richard Petty, Dale Earnhardt, Gordon, each of them has inspired those racing against them to reach higher."

After the race, an upset Gordon said, "He body-slammed me pretty good and I got pretty mad at him. There was no reason for him to slam me." With a track record like theirs, there's sure to be more Gordon vs. Wallace excitement to come.

Faces In The Rearview Mirror

As the DuPont Chevy speeds toward Victory Lane, Jeff Gordon can expect to see any one of these competitors on his back bumper, gunning for glory in the Winston Cup series.

Johnny Benson

Johnny Benson won the Winston Cup Rookie of the Year award in 1996, but didn't find success as quickly as Jeff Gordon, the 1993 Rookie of the Year. However, in the years following his remarkable rookie campaign, Benson has recorded several high points against the best drivers in the sport, including a memorable battle against Gordon for the pole at the TranSouth Financial 400 in 1999. Gordon won the pole, but it took what Gordon called an "unbelievable lap" to hold off the hard-driving Benson.

Trying For The Top 10

Johnny Benson has come close to finishing in the top-10 in the points standings twice in his Winston Cup career. He was 13th in 2000 and 11th in 1997.

Johnny Benson (Eagle One) is just behind Jeff Gordon, as is Jeremy Mayfield (Mobil) at the NAPA Auto Parts 500 in April of 2001.

Benson can be counted on to deliver a tough challenge each and every week, even when he doesn't have a sponsor to back him! He drove a plain white car during the Pepsi 400 in 2000 after sponsorship fell through for his No. 10 Pontiac.

Benson once drove for the powerful multi-car Jack Roush racing team, but left them at the end of the 1999 for a smaller racing team. He is currently sponsored by Valvoline, a company formerly known for its long association with Mark Martin. If Benson continues his climb to the top of the NASCAR standings, he may prove to be as equal a challenger to Gordon as Mark Martin is.

Bobby Labonte

Gordon leads the pack, but Bobby Labonte (left) is catching up!

AP/WWP

In 1993, Bobby Labonte battled Jeff Gordon for the Winston Cup Rookie of the Year award. Today, he's battling Gordon for Winston Cup championships.

Behind the wheel of his Interstate Batteries green machine, Labonte was the model of consistency in 2000. He won four races on his way to the Winston Cup championship, but also had 15 top-five finishes. Consistency runs in the family. Bobby's older brother Terry is a two-time Winston Cup champion. The Labonte brothers are the only siblings in Winston Cup history to win championships.

A native of Corpus Christi, Texas, Labonte grew up watching Terry tear up the local racetracks. Soon, young Bobby was also behind the wheel.

Labonte found success in the Busch series, where he was crowned champion in 1990.

The Heavy Burden Of Success

When Bobby Labonte accepted the 2000 Winston Cup championship trophy, he nearly dropped it! "That thing is heavier than it looks," said Labonte.

Labonte and Gordon share a bit of Busch history. After Gordon left Bill Davis' Ford team to drive Chevrolets for Hendrick, Davis picked Labonte to be the driver for his first Winston Cup team. Now a superstar for Joe Gibbs Racing, Labonte has his sights set on a second championship.

Sterling Marlin

Jeff Gordon makes multi-victory seasons look easy, but in the ultra-competitive Winston Cup Series, wins are tough to come by. Sterling Marlin proved this by going 278 races without a single checkered flag. Marlin picked a doozy of a race for his first win – the 1994 Daytona 500.

Sterling Martin (No. 40) and Gordon are neck and neck at the Food City 500 at Bristol Motor Speedway in March of 2001.

Marlin turned in another sterling performance the next year at the 1995 Daytona 500, when he became only the third driver to win the race in consecutive years. Since then, Marlin has added more victories to his total, and has even challenged Jeff Gordon in the points race for the Winston Cup championship. Gordon was still a boy when Marlin was named Rookie of the Year in 1983, an honor bestowed upon Gordon a decade later. Today, despite the gap in their ages, both drivers are stock car veterans.

Mark Martin

Martin On Gordon

Mark Martin doesn't like it one bit that the fans boos Jeff Gordon. Of Gordon, he once said, "He's a fine fellow and it hurts me to hear him booed because he's good."

With three second-place points finishes in his stellar Winston Cup career, Mark Martin is overdue for his first championship season. Win or lose, Martin is one of the few drivers able to compete with Jeff Gordon for the checkered flag on a weekly basis.

At the 1998 Goody's 500, Martin's win stopped Gordon from making history as the first driver of the modern era to win five races in a row. That was just one of many exciting clashes between Martin and Gordon that year. During one stretch of the 1998 season, Martin and Gordon raced to neck and neck finishes three weeks in a row. Martin's statistics – including seven wins – may have been good enough to win a championship in other years, but Gordon's amazing 13-win season left Martin with runner-up status at the conclusion of the 1998 season.

Gordon leads Mark Martin (Valvoline) at the Country Music Television 300 at New Hampshire International Speedway in August of 1998.

Martin holds the record for all-time victories (45) on the Busch Grand National circuit. In Martin's 2000 Busch series finale, Gordon spoiled the farewell with a first-place finish. It was also Gordon's last race in the Busch competition. "I'm tickled I was able to battle with a guy like Mark in my last race," said Gordon. Their days of racing in the Busch Series behind them, Martin and Gordon still have many years ahead of them to do battle on the Winston Cup circuit.

Steve Park

Steve Park's journey to the top of the NASCAR standings has been anything but a walk in the park. After struggling through 76 starts without a win, Park finally brought victory to his boss Dale Earnhardt at Watkins Glen in 2000. The victory at The Glen ended Jeff Gordon's streak of six consecutive road-course wins. Park also held off Gordon to score an emotional victory at the 2001 Dura Lube 400 – the first race held after Earnhardt's untimely death. "I had tears

Jon Ferrey/Allsport

Steve Park (Pennzoil) is close behind Gordon at Bristol Motor Speedway in 2000.

coming down those last couple of laps," said Park. Gordon wasn't mad at finishing behind Park. "I'm really happy for the gang at Dale Earnhardt Inc.," said Gordon of Park's win. The Intimidator may be gone, but his DEI protégé is capable of racing alongside Gordon for years to come.

Ricky Rudd

There are only a select few drivers who have competed long enough and consistently enough to record at least 700 Winston Cup starts. The names of these drivers are some of the most legendary in the sport. Richard Petty. Darrell Waltrip. Bobby Allison.

And don't forget Ricky Rudd.

Stock car veteran Ricky Rudd holds a Winston Cup record of 16 consecutive seasons with at least one victory. Rudd's most famous exchange with Jeff Gordon came at the 1999 Daytona 500, the race remembered for Gordon's fearless pass between race leader Rusty Wallace's No. 2 and Rudd's lapped and ailing car that was slowly completing the race to collect Winston Cup points. Prior to that event, Rudd won the 1997 Brickyard 400, a race that Gordon is no stranger to winning.

Gordon has shown that he can string together consistently excellent seasons much like Rudd has. "That string is amazing. You could see the fire in him today," said Gordon after Rudd extended his streak of 16 seasons (1983-1998) with at least one win each. Although Rudd's streak has since ended, the competitive fires still burn within him, making him a threat to start a new streak at any moment.

Gordon edges out Ricky Rudd for the victory at the Kmart 400 at Michigan International Speedway in 2001.

Young Guns Of Winston

Jeff Gordon is still young and taking NASCAR by storm – and he promises to keep up the good work. But his rookie season is far in the past, and a whole new crop of rookies is ready to take on the nickname of "Wonder Boy."

Kevin Harvick

It can't be easy to find opportunity in the midst of a deep tragedy. But that's what happened to Kevin Harvick, the driver who's taken on the task of filling NASCAR's most famous driver's seat.

When the 2001 season began, Harvick was supposed to run only a few races in the Winston Cup Series. During a stellar first season in the Busch Series the previous year, the young Californian (he's in his mid-20s) scored an amazing three wins and won Rookie of the Year honors. That success prepared him for the big leagues in the Winston Cup, under the tutelage of the great Dale Earnhardt.

David Leeds/ALLSPORT

It's a photo finish, and Kevin Harvick beats Jeff Gordon at the Cracker Barrel 500 at Atlanta Motor Speedway in 2001.

But Earnhardt's tragic death at the 2001 Daytona 500 literally put Harvick in the driver's seat. Richard Childress Racing selected him to drive Earnhardt's Chevrolet Monte Carlo for the rest of the 2001 season. For a rookie just beginning to get his feet wet in the big leagues, that was a tall order to fill.

But Harvick proved himself more than capable in March of 2001 at the Cracker Barrel 500 at Atlanta Motor Speedway, when he was able to zoom ahead of none other than Jeff Gordon and win the checkered flag by a fraction of a second. It was only the third race of Harvick's Winston Cup career, and his win put the No. 29 Goodwrench Chevrolet into the hearts and minds of fans everywhere.

Casey Atwood

Team owner Ray Evernham sure knows how to pick 'em. Years ago, he was the crew chief for Jeff Gordon – the Wonder Boy who refused to lose. Now he has a new protégé in Casey Atwood, a rookie who promises to give Gordon a run for his money.

Jonathan Ferrey/ALLSPORT

Casey Atwood helms the No. 19 Dodge Dealers Intrepid.

Nashville native Atwood got an early start in racing, starting with go-carts as a young boy, and moved his way up to the Craftsman Truck series when the ink was barely dry on his driver's license. Then he moved on to the Busch series, where he made a name for himself in 1998 by becoming the youngest driver ever to win a Busch Series event, at the age of 18 years and 10 months.

Of Atwood, Evernham says, "[W]hen you see somebody who is doing well in every kind of car he drives and he's only 19, it can't be experience. It has to be talent."

So does Atwood's bright, young star image sound familiar to Gordon fans? Of course. But Evernham says it shouldn't. "Casey won't be treated like Jeff Gordon because he's not Jeff Gordon," he says.

Maybe not. But Gordon is sure to see Atwood's No. 19 Dodge Dealers Intrepid in his rearview mirror a time or two in the seasons to come.

> ### Don't You Have School Tomorrow?
>
> When Atwood was in Las Vegas in 2001, the manager of a car rental lot thought he was too young to drive, and almost refused to give him the keys to a rental car.

Andy Houston

It's not often that a determined young driver jumps right from the Craftsman Truck series right into Winston Cup competition, driving the No. 96 McDonald's Ford. But Andy Houston has done just that, and his incredible record in the Craftsman series has proved him worthy. After all, Houston's got racing in his family tree!

The son of legendary Busch series driver Tommy Houston (and the cousin of Teresa Earnhardt, Dale Earnhardt's widow), this North Carolinian broke into the Craftsman Series in 1998, pulling himself up into an impressive 12th place that rookie year. As if that weren't enough, Houston ended his

Andy Houston spins out at the Cracker Barrel 500 at Atlanta Motor Speedway in March of 2001. Buckshot Jones (No. 44) is in the background.

Craftsman stint in 2000 by making it into the top ten 18 times in 24 races and finishing in third place in the points race!

When he first appeared in a Winston Cup race in 2000, the 30-year-old Houston amazed crowds and drivers alike when he qualified in 35th position, yet sped up to sixth and surely would have finished higher, had engine failure not knocked him out of the race.

Kurt Busch

Ever since he raced his father's dwarf car near his hometown of Las Vegas in the 1980s, Kurt Busch has dreamed of a shot at the Winston Cup series. Now he's got it.

Kurt Busch drives the No. 97 Sharpie/Rubbermaid Ford for Jack Roush Racing.

Chris Stanford/ALLSPORT

With the experienced Jack Roush organization behind him and a great record in the Craftsman series (he finished in second place in 2000), Busch is ready to spring into the Winston Cup and the No. 97 Sharpie/Rubbermaid Ford with a vengeance.

Busch is still in shock from his career move. "Everything has just moved so quickly for me," he says. "From moving from the West Coast to Michigan [for the Craftsman series] and then finding out in mid-summer I was going to Winston Cup. It's all been sort of overwhelming." But with a brand-new sponsor and the will to win, you can be sure that Busch will make a name for himself in his new venue.

Jason Leffler

When Jason Leffler made his debut in the Busch series in 2000, the native Californian impressed fans everywhere by placing 20th in that year's point standings. With a debut like that, it looked as if he might have a great Busch career ahead of him. It's not every rookie who manages to win three poles and amass four top-ten finishes, as Leffler did in 2000.

Jason Leffler shows who's number one as he leads the pack in his No. 1 Dodge at the Cracker Barrel 500 at Atlanta Motor speedway in March of 2001.

But Leffler decided to go for the gold when Chip Ganassi Racing lured him into driving the No. 1 Cingular Wireless Dodge in the Winston Cup series. Now, Leffler looks forward to years of living up to his car's number. "My goal has always been to race Winston Cup," he says, "and now I will be able to pursue that dream."

NASCAR® Legends

Since NASCAR was founded in 1948, hundreds of drivers have dreamed of a career racing the tracks in the NASCAR circuit. However, only a select few have had the determination to push the envelope no matter what the cost. Here's a look at some of those legendary drivers.

Bobby Allison

Hometown: *Hueytown, Alabama*
Birthdate: *December 3, 1937*
Years Raced: *25*
Starts: *718*
Wins: *85*
Pole Positions: *59*
Retired: *1988*

Buck Baker

Hometown: *Charlotte, North Carolina*
Birthdate: *March 4, 1919*
Years Raced: *26*
Starts: *636*
Wins: *46*
Pole Positions: *44*
Retired: *1976*

Buddy Baker

Hometown: *Charlotte, North Carolina*
Birthdate: *January 25, 1941*
Years Raced: *34*
Starts: *699*
Wins: *19*
Pole Positions: *40*
Retired: *1994*

Neil Bonnett

Hometown: *Bessemer, Alabama*
Birthdate: *July 30, 1946*
Years Raced: *18*
Starts: *363*
Wins: *18*
Pole Positions: *20*
Deceased: *February 11, 1994*

Dale Earnhardt

Hometown: *Kannapolis, North Carolina*
Birthdate: *April 29, 1951*
Years Raced: *26*
Starts: *675*
Wins: *76*
Pole Positions: *22*
Deceased: *February 18, 2001*

Tim Flock

Hometown: *Fort Payne, Alabama*
Birthdate: *May 11, 1924*
Years Raced: *13*
Starts: *187*
Wins: *39*
Pole Positions: *39*
Retired: *1961*

A.J. Foyt

Hometown: *Houston, Texas*
Birthdate: *January 16, 1935*
Years Raced: *31*
Starts: *128*
Wins: *7*
Pole Positions: *10*
Retired: *1994*

Ned Jarrett

Hometown: *Newton, North Carolina*
Birthdate: *October 12, 1932*
Years Raced: *13*
Starts: *352*
Wins: *50*
Pole Positions: *35*
Retired: *1966*

Junior Johnson

Hometown: *Ronda, North Carolina*
Birthdate: *June 28, 1931*
Years Raced: *14*
Starts: *313*
Wins: *50*
Pole Positions: *47*
Retired: *1966*

Alan Kulwicki

Hometown: *Greenfield, Wisconsin*
Birthdate: *December 14, 1954*
Years Raced: *9*
Starts: *207*
Wins: *5*
Pole Positions: *24*
Deceased: *April 1, 1993*

Benny Parsons

Hometown: *Detroit, Michigan*
Birthdate: *July 12, 1941*
Years Raced: *21*
Starts: *526*
Wins: *21*
Pole Positions: *20*
Retired: *1988*

David Pearson

Hometown: *Spartanburg, South Carolina*
Birthdate: *December 22, 1934*
Years Raced: *27*
Starts: *574*
Wins: *105*
Pole Positions: *113*
Retired: *1986*

Lee Petty

Hometown: *Level Cross, North Carolina*
Birthdate: *March 14, 1914*
Years Raced: *16*
Starts: *427*
Wins: *54*
Pole Positions: *18*
Retired: *1964*
Deceased: *April 5, 2000*

Richard Petty

Hometown: *Level Cross, North Carolina*
Birthdate: *July 2, 1937*
Years Raced: *35*
Starts: *1184*
Wins: *200*
Pole Positions: *126*
Retired: *1992*

Fireball Roberts

Hometown: *Daytona Beach, Florida*
Birthdate: *January 20, 1929*
Years Raced: *15*
Starts: *206*
Wins: *33*
Pole Positions: *35*
Deceased: *July 2, 1964*

Herb Thomas

Hometown: *Hartnett County, North Carolina*
Birthdate: *April 6, 1923*
Years Raced: *10*
Starts: *230*
Wins: *48*
Pole Positions: *38*
Retired: *1956*
Deceased: *August 9, 2000*

Darrell Waltrip

Hometown: *Franklin, Tennessee*
Birthdate: *February 5, 1947*
Years Raced: *30*
Starts: *749*
Wins: *84*
Pole Positions: *59*
Retired: *2000*

Joe Weatherly

Hometown: *Norfolk, Virginia*
Birthdate: *May 29, 1922*
Years Raced: *12*
Starts: *230*
Wins: *25*
Pole Positions: *19*
Deceased: *January 19, 1964*

Cale Yarborough

Hometown: *Timmonsville, South Carolina*
Birthdate: *March 27, 1939*
Years Raced: *31*
Starts: *559*
Wins: *83*
Pole Positions: *70*
Retired: *1988*

BEHIND THE
SCENES OF RACING

History Of NASCAR®

Stock car racing's roots stretch back to the moonshiners and bootleggers who needed superior driving skills to avoid the authorities and transport their unlawful product throughout the rural Southern United States. These daredevil drivers later found their skills useful in another thrilling avenue – stock car racing.

Back in the early days of NASCAR, there were many organizations billing themselves as sanctioning bodies of the sport. It seemed that every organization had its own champions, standards and rules, and those were just from the legitimate organizations. Many more races were run by unscrupulous promoters who overlooked flagrant cheating by popular drivers, advertised huge prizes that didn't exist and frequently sneaked away while a race was in progress, taking all the ticket money with them.

Between the moonshine runners and the crooked promoters, racing seemed doomed to be an outlaw sport forever. It was against this cultural backdrop that William Henry Getty France, or "Big Bill" as he was known, got his start.

Bobby Sall's car flips during a pre-NASCAR era race at Daytona Beach, Florida, on March 2, 1936. Sall was rendered unconscious but had no other serious injuries.

Big Bill And The Birth Of NASCAR®

Bill France was an expert mechanic and racer who moved to Daytona Beach, Florida, in 1934. Daytona already had a long history as a racing town; in the early days of the automobile, many land-speed records were set on Daytona's long, flat beaches. As the speeds grew higher, the Daytona Chamber of Commerce, hoping to lure even more race tourists, set up a 4.1-mile course on the beach.

> ## Red Brings Home The Green!
>
> In 1948, Robert "Red" Byron won the first official NASCAR race. In 1949, he went on to win two more races, becoming the first winner of what would later be known as the Winston Cup.

The first two races held on this course, in 1936 and 1937, were far from organized, so in 1938, France was given the opportunity to organize the race. He attracted many good drivers, kept careful count of the number of laps each driver completed and made an attractive profit. Thereafter, France continued to promote the annual beach race.

Bill France in 1984, after receiving the Patrick Jacquemart Trophy in recognition for his contributions to auto racing.

In late 1947, France met with a mix of promoters, drivers and mechanics to form the National Association of Stock Car Auto Racing – NASCAR. France was named president, and wasted no time in exerting his power for the good of the sport.

NASCAR's first race, held on February 15, 1948, at Daytona Beach, featured nearly 50 drivers and was won by Red Byron. After 52 races were held from Florida to Pennsylvania, NASCAR's debut season was celebrated as a success.

The 1950s And 1960s

Beginning in the 1950s, NASCAR racing began to change in several ways. First, NASCAR enjoyed tremendous growth, sanctioning races before thousands of fans on tracks all over the country. Another sign of the popularity of NASCAR racing was the paving and expansion of racetracks. The first asphalt track was built in Darlington, South Carolina, in 1950. Its first race, billed as the Southern 500, was a truly spectacular affair witnessed by about 20,000 spectators.

Fans came out to watch the Firecracker 250 at Daytona Beach on July 4, 1960.

AP/WWP

In 1951, the era of automobile-industry sponsorship began when Marshall Teague, who won the opening race of the season in a Hudson Hornet, contracted with an appreciative Hudson for cars and parts. Later that year, Bill France opened the door to a relationship between NASCAR and automobile manufacturers by staging a race in Detroit during the city's 250th anniversary celebration. Soon, car manufacturers were waging their corporate battles through NASCAR racers.

Car owner Carl Kiekaefer is largely credited with introducing innovations in the mid-1950s that are now familiar parts of the NASCAR scene. These included placing sponsor names on cars, transporting race cars on trucks, maintaining a stable of multiple cars and having a professional pit crew dressed in matching uniforms.

Paving The Way

The old-time dirt tracks were slowly paved over in favor of the new, high-speed, asphalt tracks. By 1969, all but five of 54 stock car races were held on asphalt tracks.

The Modern Era

When reading through the NASCAR record book, the term "modern era" is often mentioned. The modern era was ushered in by Bill France Jr. in 1972 when a new, shorter schedule was unveiled. Bill France Jr. had taken the reins to NASCAR over from his father, and immediately set out to reestablish NASCAR's dominance in the world of stock car racing.

He devised a new, shorter schedule so that teams no longer had to race throughout the country, multiple times a week. Fewer races a season, however, now make some of the older season records nearly untouchable. With a NASCAR season now only 36 points races long, it is doubtful that any driver will ever again win 27 races in a single season, as could be done in the old days.

Driver safety was an issue in this period, and several rules were instituted in an effort to curb dangerous racing speeds. Carburetor restrictor plates appeared in 1970 and the following year saw a limit on engine sizes. Other regulations that changed the face of NASCAR racing included the introduction of cars with power steering, reduced wheelbase requirements and smaller carburetors, all in the 1980s.

Perhaps the biggest single change in NASCAR's fortunes came when R.J. Reynolds (maker of Winston cigarettes) stepped in as a major sponsor of the sport in the early 1970s. This marked the first major NASCAR sponsorship from a company that did not produce automobile products. Soon, other non-automotive companies followed suit. This was good

AP/WWP

Richard Petty (No. 43) defeats David Pearson (No. 2) at Michigan International Speedway in 1975 for his 173rd NASCAR career win.

news for NASCAR racing because more sponsorships meant that race winnings (called purses) could grow even higher.

As corporations took greater interest in NASCAR, more and more of the races took corporate names: the Southern 500 became the Heinz 500, Charlotte's World 600 became the Coca-Cola 600 and so forth.

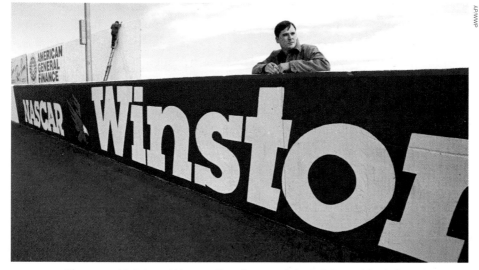

AP/WWP

There wouldn't be a Winston Cup if it wasn't for R.J. Reynolds and its sponsorship of NASCAR racing. Track employee Jeff Cottle takes a break from putting up new billboards at Charlotte Motor Speedway in 1997.

But even more importantly, the R.J. Reynolds contract came with more than just money: a television package that provided for taped national broadcasts of NASCAR races. Television was crucial to the expansion of racing's popularity through the 1970s and 1980s. The age of taped broadcasts and live "final lap" break-away coverage officially ended with the first live broadcast of a major NASCAR event from start to finish – the 1979 Daytona 500. Within a few years of that memorable event, cable and network television combined to carry every major NASCAR race, completing NASCAR's transition from a regional draw to a national sport.

The 1990s

In the 1990s, NASCAR's popularity reached an all-time high, seeing new tracks built all over the United States and even exhibition races held in Japan. New innovations included the prevalence of multi-car teams, the use of computers in the pits and increased specialization of crew members.

AP/WWP

The New Millennium

With multi-million dollar race purses and official merchandise sales in excess of $1 billion annually, NASCAR racing seems poised for even greater heights. How will advancing technology affect NASCAR racing? What other countries will jump on the NASCAR bandwagon? Will any more new series be started? The answers to these questions will be part of the exciting world of NASCAR racing in the new millennium!

Dale Jarrett was the last Winston Cup winner of the 20th century.

Winston Cup Overview

Baseball has the Major Leagues, basketball has the NBA, and racing has the NASCAR Winston Cup series. The most popular and competitive racing circuit in the country gives millions of fans thrills every week on some of the best racetracks in the world.

You know the names – Gordon, Earnhardt Jr., Labonte, Wallace, Stewart. These are the mega-stars of NASCAR racing, and the Winston Cup Series has them! Recognized as the major league of stock car racing, the Winston Cup series has become one of the most popular – and profitable – sports attraction in the country, drawing fans to tracks and televisions in record numbers. That's why, when you're talking about NASCAR, you might as well be talking about the Winston Cup series!

At A Track Near You

Winston Cup races take place nearly every single weekend between February and November. With a whopping 39 points and non-points events scheduled for 2001 alone, Winston Cup drivers and fans alike are kept pretty busy!

Some of these events have become "old friends" to legions of NASCAR fans: the Coca-Cola 600, the Southern 500, the Daytona 500, the Winston Select and the Cracker Barrel 500 are among the highlights of the year.

AP/WWP

Jeff Gordon pops the cork after a win at Las Vegas Motor Speedway on March 4, 2001.

Traditionally, races are held around the same time and at the same track every year, so fans can look forward to kicking off the year with the Daytona 500 in February and closing out with the NAPA 500 at Atlanta Motor Speedway in November. But NASCAR's recent television deal has caused some tinkering with the traditional schedule. The Winston Cup series visits Chicago and Kansas City for the first time in 2001, and more changes may be on the way.

Track Talk

There are four different kinds of tracks that host Winston Cup Series races. First, there are the big bruisers – the **superspeedways**. Daytona and Talladega are the only two superspeedways that appear on the Winston Cup schedule. They are each at least 2-1/2 miles long and feature long straightaways that allow drivers to reach speeds close to 200 mph. Thanks to these high speeds, cars must use restrictor plates on these tracks, which cut down their speed and power. Thus, cars tend to race in packs as they "draft" behind one another.

Most of the Winston Cup tracks are **intermediate tracks**, from one to two miles long. These feature a combination of speed and some bumping and braking. Still, each of the tracks drives differently based on characteristics like banking and turns.

AP/WWP

The race begins as the sun sets on Richmond International Raceway (a short track) on September 7, 1996, at the Miller 400.

Next are the **short tracks**, which are less than a mile in length. Drivers can really fly on these courses, when they aren't braking into a turn or bumping each other! If you see a 10-car crash on TV, chances are it was on a short track, such as Bristol Motor Speedway or Martinsville Speedway.

Sears Point Raceway and Watkins Glen International Speedway are examples of **road courses**. These tracks are a real workout, rife with dips and all kinds of hairpin turns. Drivers usually have a sore brake foot after driving on one of these!

Because each type of track demands something different from the cars, teams must modify race cars to best suit the track conditions. Springs, shocks, tires, brakes and aerodynamic flow all will be adjusted depending on whether the driver is on a superspeedway or a road course. These adjustments are called the "setup" of a car. Teams sometimes will have several different cars tailor-made for particular tracks.

Jeff Gordon leads Sterling Martin on the road course at Sears Point Raceway in 2000.

AP/WWP

Rules And Regulations

Most of the rules that distinguish the Winston Cup series from other NASCAR races have to do with car specifications. Inspectors pore over cars before the race and literally pick them apart afterward to verify that the cars adhere to NASCAR's guidelines. These guidelines cover every detail you can imagine – engine volume and configuration, body details, seat belts and more.

Lights, Camera, Fight!

The 1979 Daytona 500 turned out to be a memorable and exciting race. Its dramatic ending included a last-lap collision and a post-race fistfight between the Allison brothers, Bobby and Donnie, and Cale Yarborough!

NASCAR officials inspect the rear spoiler of Dave Marcis' car at Daytona International Speedway in 2001 as crew chief Bob Marcis (blue shirt) looks on. Bob is Dave's nephew.

Winston Cup cars must weigh at least 3,400 pounds, have a wheelbase of 110 inches and a roof height of 51 inches. Engines can have a maximum volume of 358 cubic inches and a compression ratio of 12:1, which translates into about 750 horsepower.

NASCAR uses pieces of metal called templates, that fit parts of every car to ensure they meet specified sizes – no body detail can be too small or too large. These tight and consistent rules mean that all the drivers are pretty much using the same technology, so races will be decided by skill, experience and determination, not equipment.

"I Could Do That!"

No, you couldn't! There's much more to Winston Cup racing than just driving fast, and not everyone can just jump in and start up a car. At the very least, you have to be 16 years old and pass a physical.

You're not likely to make it to the Winston Cup circuit – and certainly can't stay there for any length of time – without years of racing experience to prove that you won't be in over your head. Unlike other sports that have minor leagues or college ranks, there's no formal system to work your way up through. Still, many of the current Winston Cup drivers cut their teeth in other racing divisions, usually the Busch circuit. Most drivers start at an early age and spend years paying their dues at local paved and dirt tracks. They've proven they have the skills and the mental toughness to race against the top drivers in the world, on the most difficult tracks, at very high speeds.

Making The Grade

Only 43 cars will actually take to the track on Winston Cup race day. That's because two days of qualifying trials take place before the big day to determine who's in and who's out.

Qualifying trials can be frantic and tense affairs. Underdogs fight for their professional lives, while Winston Cup veterans like Dale Jarrett and Bobby Labonte want to place as high as possible to ensure a good position on race day.

The qualifying trials take place over two days, with the top 25 drivers on the first day automatically making the cut. The rest of the field is decided through a trial on the second day. At that time, drivers who didn't make the top 25 can go through it again or stand on their first-day time and take the chance that no one will beat them out the second day. At the end of the two days, the 36 fastest drivers make the cut, seven get provisional entries and the

Gordon and Ricky Rudd (Texaco) lead the pack to the green flag at the start of the Kmart 400 at Michigan Speedway on June 10, 2001.

rest go home. The goal of the provisional entries is to ensure that a star driver who had a bad qualifying run still gets into the race.

The driver with the fastest qualifying time is the "pole winner" or "pole sitter." On race day, that driver will start the race in the front row, on the inside position, while the other drivers will start in two columns based on where they ranked in the qualifying rounds.

And The Winner Is . . .

At the end of every Winston Cup Series race, drivers (and owners) are awarded points. These points are the basis of the standings and are used to determine the Winston Cup Series champion at the end of the season.

NASCAR has used several different point systems over the years, but the current system has been in place since 1975. A driver earns 175 points for winning a Winston Cup race, with the next five drivers receiving five fewer points. The next six drivers earn four fewer points, and the rest of the field wins three fewer points.

Drivers can also earn bonus points. Those who lead at least one lap at any point in the race get five bonus points, while the driver who leads the most laps gets five more bonus points. So in a given race, the winner will get at least 180 points (175 for winning, 5 for leading the last lap) and could get 185 points if he or she led the most laps that day.

AP/WWP

The checkered flag belongs to Gordon at the California Speedway in 1997.

How does NASCAR keep track of all those cars and where they place? NASCAR timing and scoring officials use transponders – small boxes mounted to the underside of cars – that transmit a signal every time the car completes a lap. In addition, each team has a scorer who keeps track of the number of laps for a car with a push-button device, or on paper. That way, if there's a discrepancy, NASCAR has it covered.

Gordon leads the field by several car lengths at New Hampshire International Speedway in 1998.

AP/WWP

The Winston Cup championship goes to the driver who has the most points at the end of the season. If two drivers are tied in points, the driver with the most wins that season is the champion; if neither has won a race, it's second-place finishes, then third-place finishes and so forth that are counted.

Team owners earn points, too, because they may use different drivers over the course of a season. Owners earn the same number of points their drivers earn for a race. Each season, the owner with the most points wins the owner's championship.

Hey, Nice Purse

These guys aren't racing just for the championship, you know!

Points

The following are the number of points a driver receives based on his or her finish in a Winston Cup race.

1 = 175	16 = 115	31 = 70
2 = 170	17 = 112	32 = 67
3 = 165	18 = 109	33 = 64
4 = 160	19 = 106	34 = 61
5 = 155	20 = 103	35 = 58
6 = 150	21 = 100	36 = 55
7 = 146	22 = 97	37 = 52
8 = 142	23 = 94	38 = 49
9 = 138	24 = 91	39 = 46
10 = 134	25 = 88	40 = 43
11 = 130	26 = 85	41 = 40
12 = 127	27 = 82	42 = 37
13 = 124	28 = 79	43 = 34
14 = 121	29 = 76	
15 = 118	30 = 73	

Racing is their livelihood and Winston Cup drivers have enjoyed larger and larger cash winnings (called purses) over the years. Drivers can expect a winner's purse as well as a percentage of television revenue for the race. Together, this comes to about 30% of a race winner's total take.

The other 70% is made up of all kinds of bonuses and awards. The 10 drivers who won the most races the previous year are eligible for the Winner's Circle program, which gives them bonus money for winning a race. Race sponsors usually put up extra prize money, while some sponsors of individual drivers will offer a contingency award if they win a race while using their product or equipment. Other awards give top dollar to race winners, top-10 finishers or points leaders, ranging anywhere from $1,000 to $10,000 or even more!

Of course, Winston Cup racing is more than big bucks and fast cars. There's the constant travel, the unending scrutiny of the media, the physical wear and tear on drivers' bodies and the very real threat of death with every race. But you can bet that today's Winston Cup drivers wouldn't want to change places with anybody!

AP/WWp

Gordon won $1 million in bonus money at Darlington Raceway in 1997.

Today's NASCAR® Headlines

NASCAR doesn't just make headlines on race weekends. Sometimes, the most interesting and dramatic events occur away from the track. Here are some of the recent stories that had Winston Cup fans buzzing.

The 2000 Winston Cup season ended with the retirement of Darrell Waltrip, a racing veteran who won three championships during a career that spanned almost 30 years on the track. The opening of the 2001 Winston Cup season saw the last race of another racing legend, but this race was a cause for mourning. The tragic death of Dale Earnhardt at the season-opening Daytona 500 cast a shadow over the entire racing community, and also brought the issue of safety to the forefront of the stock car racing world.

Stock car racing is a thrilling occupation, but with speed comes danger, and while the tracks have always had their share of pile-ups and accidents, a string of recent fatalities has made safety an issue on everybody's minds.

AP/WWP

Darrell Waltrip's (left) retirement and Dale Earnhardt's (right) death have left a void in the sport.

A Question Of Safety

New Hampshire International Speedway made headlines in 2000 after Adam Petty – a fourth-generation NASCAR racer – and Kenny Irwin Jr. were killed in similar accidents on Turn 3 of the track within weeks of each other. In the interest of safety, NASCAR mandated the use of restrictor plates during the 2000 Dura Lube 300, the first Winston Cup race held at the Loudon, New Hampshire, track after the accidents.

Restrictor plates have long been a thorny issue with drivers. A restrictor plate is a metal device that restricts the flow of air into the car. This cuts down the horsepower, making the car go slower as a result.

Awesome Bill's Awesome Record

Back before restrictor plates were used at Talladega Superspeedway, Bill Elliott set a track (and Winston Cup) qualifying record with a speed of over 212 miles per hour!

The plates are regularly used on the superspeedways of Daytona and Talladega, where speeds in excess of 190 mph can occur. When a car travels that fast, it becomes a danger to fans in the stands, should it become airborne and leave the track. While the plates make races safer for fans in the stands, they can cause chaos on the track for drivers, who get bunched together and are forced to race in tight packs because they are all racing at similar speeds.

It's hard to believe that this little plate could have so many enemies, but dozens of stock car racers don't like restrictor plates and the tight racing conditions they create.

"I hate restrictor-plate races, all of them," Dale Earnhardt was once quoted as saying, but drivers have learned to make the best of the congested driving conditions. "I'd say the last 15 laps here were the most horrifying and the most exciting I've ever run in my life," said Jeff Gordon after a restrictor plate race at Talladega. "I put the 24 car in spots I've never put it before."

A Winston Cup official holds a restrictor plate up for inspection at Talladega Superspeedway.

An April 2001, race at Talladega almost became more well-known for what didn't happen at the track than for what did. NASCAR officials made multiple changes in the rules that angered some of the drivers, who felt the new rules compromised their safety.

Rumors of a driver boycott spread in the weeks leading up to the race. Bobby Labonte went so far as to imply that some sponsors would not mind their drivers sitting out the Talladega race.

The hard feelings stemmed from the preponderance of multi-car wrecks at the superspeedway. "More than likely when you go to other tracks, the chances of getting caught in a wreck are slim. But at Talladega, they might be 50/50," said Michael Waltrip.

Unintimidated

Kevin Harvick, who now drives Dale Earnhardt's car, feels the same way about restrictor plates as the Intimidator did. "We race cars for a living and if [the officials] don't want to go fast, they need to find something else to do as far as I'm concerned," said Harvick.

Even though there were hard feelings, the drivers knew they had a job to do. "I'm not a big fan of these rules. But I'll be in Talladega because that's my job," said Bobby Labonte's big brother Terry. In the end, every driver showed up for race day – Bobby Labonte included – and no major accidents spoiled the race.

A safety device that has been even more closely scrutinized than the restrictor plate is the head and neck support (HANS) device. Already used in other forms of racing, the HANS device was slow to gain support on the Winston Cup circuit. Earnhardt's death changed that.

Michael Waltrip, a driver for Earnhardt's DEI team, began using the device shortly after his boss's death. "I didn't have any problem with [the HANS]. I actually like it a lot. I like it better than without it. I put it on and I loved it," said Waltrip.

Other drivers were initially wary of the device deemed by some to be cumbersome and a liability if the driver needed to escape the car quickly. "I've been working with the HANS device. I haven't been able to make it work for me," said Jeff Gordon early in the 2001 season. As the season progressed, Gordon had a change of heart. "When I first put one on, it wasn't even close. But we got one custom fitted and I won't race on a big track without it," said Gordon.

AP/WWP

The HANS device is being used more and more by safety-conscious drivers.

Jeff Gordon takes a pit stop from promoting the Tropicana 400
at Chicagoland Speedway to sign an autograph for a fan.

A few drivers have been outspoken critics of the device. Mark Martin has said, "I wouldn't wear a HANS device for anything." NASCAR has yet to make the HANS device a mandatory piece of safety equipment, although NASCAR president Mike Helton encourages use of the device.

Sweet Home, Chicago

With the increased scrutiny of track safety, the introduction of two new tracks to the Winston Cup series brought positive press to NASCAR's speedways. Chicagoland Speedway in Joliet, Illinois, and Kansas Speedway in Kansas City both celebrated their inaugural season in 2001.

To help get fans "revved up" for the new Illinois speedway, Jeff Gordon answered phones in the ticket office at the Chicagoland track. Gordon also was on hand in March to unveil the Tropicana 400 logo. "All of the Winston Cup drivers have been looking forward to racing at Chicagoland Speedway for a while now," said Gordon.

Running Down A Dream

One driver racing on these new Winston Cup tracks was an unfamiliar sight to the male-dominated sport of stock car racing. On June 10, 2001, Shawna Robinson became the first woman to start in a Winston Cup race since Patty Moise's 1989 Talladega effort. Robinson's schedule planned to take her to the California Speedway, Michigan Speedway, Indianapolis Motor Speedway and Atlanta Motor Speedway, as well as the new tracks in Chicago and Kansas.

> ### Ward Burton On Shawna Robinson
>
> "Walking around the pits, she was a female. Strapped in the car, she was a driver. She took as good as she gave. That says a lot right there."

Robinson was optimistic about her chances on the new tracks. "Being a new track, there's an even playing field with test times and getting the car set up," she said. After failing to make the field in her first 2001 attempt at California Speedway, Robinson rebounded at Michigan Speedway where she qualified for the Kmart 400 and raced to a respectable 34th-place finish.

AP/WWP

Shawna Robinson achieved her goal of making a Winston Cup start in 2001.

Robinson, a Rookie of the Year runner-up in the Busch Series, where she is also the only woman to win a pole, has long had the sport in her blood. She started out racing when she was just a girl. "[W]e spent about as much time running mini-bikes as we did playing with Barbies," said Robinson, who stuck with her passion and began serious competition in her teen years.

Many think the time has come for women on the race

track. "If Shawna could run in the top 10 . . . she would have the largest sponsorship potential our sport has ever seen," said promoter H.A. "Humpy" Wheeler. "Racing would end up on the cover of *Time* magazine," he went on. "It would transcend the sport."

Jeff Gordon expressed similar sentiments. "I always have been a believer that it doesn't matter, you know, male, female, what color your skin is – if you've got the ability and the talents," you can drive in a Winston Cup race, said Gordon in an interview with Larry King.

Why is Bobby Labonte (left) laughing? Maybe because reports of his death were greatly exaggerated.

AP/WWP

Dead Man Driving

In her first attempt of the season, Robinson's dreams were dashed by a faulty automotive rear end that prevented her from qualifying for the NAPA Auto Parts 500 at California Speedway. The pole was won by Bobby Labonte, who had an even more distressing piece of news relayed to him at the event. Word was going around that he was dead!

Labonte was the victim of a rumor that said the reigning Winston Cup champion died in a car accident. The report was picked up by several news sources and caused much grief for Labonte and his family. "It's been kind of rough. My wife is the maddest she's ever been, but she's glad, too. It's unfortunate that my parents, her parents, a lot of friends and family have to deal with what somebody started," said Labonte.

The Road Warrior

Tony Stewart made headlines with his grueling doubleheader on May 27, 2001, when he drove in both the Indy Racing League's Indianapolis 500 and NASCAR's Coca-Cola 600. Considered by fans and sportswriters as either crazy or courageous, Stewart's doubleheader was also a charitable event. Stewart pledged to donate $100 for every lap he completed to Kyle Petty's Victory Junction Gang Camp. After The Home Depot, Joe Gibbs Racing and Target Chip Ganassi Racing matched the sum, Stewart raised $240,000 for the charity. "That gave both of these races a purpose, rather than being something selfish that I wanted to do for my personal goals and personal dreams," said

AP/WWP

Stewart. "We were able to do something very productive tonight and help a lot of good kids who deserve this."

Stewart had tried the dynamic double in 1999, but did not complete the Coca-Cola race because of fatigue. With the aid of a personal trainer, Stewart was better prepared for the 1,100 laps on his second attempt. Stewart raced to a sixth-place finish at Indy. After taking a jet flight from Indiana to North Carolina, Stewart settled in behind the wheel of his No. 20 Home Depot Pontiac, which he raced to a third-place finish, even after spinning out early in the race.

After completing the Indianapolis 500, Tony Stewart prepares to take his flight to the Coca-Cola 600.

Big Time: Midget Racing

No, it's not racing for short people. Midget racing is the oldest continuous form of auto racing in the United States, and it's the type of racing that put Jeff Gordon on the road to NASCAR glory.

Jeff Gordon fans know that Gordon got his start in racing at age 5, when he began racing quarter midget cars. But how many of us really know all that much about midget racing?

The Same, But Different

Midget race cars look a lot like dune buggies – the wheels are completely exposed (aficionados and those in the know use the term "open wheel"), the chassis is low to the ground and the driver's compartment is wide open. They're even driven on sand! Well, okay, they are driven on dirt – most midget races take place on dirt tracks.

Midget drivers dress the same as NASCAR drivers, but boy, are their vehicles different!

But midget racers have engines that are far more powerful than that of a dune buggy – most have a horsepower of about 300, along with a four-cylinder engine. And they can reach approximate speeds of 170 mph on the straight-aways (and about 140 mph going through turns). Fans enjoy watching midget racing because the small cars get up to tremendous speeds, and the open cockpit allows spectators to see exactly what the driver is doing during the race.

Although several of today's hot NASCAR drivers got their start racing midgets, there is hardly any age restriction in the sport. Kids as young as 5 can race quarter midgets (a smaller midget racer) and some midget racers never grow up – they keep on racing well into their 50s.

Long, Long Ago . . .

The first midget races were held in June of 1933 in California. The midget racers evolved from cars that raced on long tracks at races like the Indianapolis 500. The early midgets were raced on small tracks (usually a quarter-mile) that provided big excitement to the fans.

Soon, midget racing became popular all over the country and fans flocked to the dirt tracks to watch them. At that time, midgets were the way to go if a driver wanted to get to the Indy 500 someday. The popularity of the sport

Many legendary drivers, such as 1958 Indianapolis 500 winner
Jimmy "Cowboy" Bryan, got their start in midget racers.

AP/WWP

Sprint car racers Donny Schatz (left) and Mark Kinser (right)
battle for the championship trophy at the 2000 Knoxville Nationals.

reached its height immediately following World War II, and crowds of more than 60,000 spectators were not unusual at some of the larger venues.

However, with the advent of television and increased competition for entertainment dollars, the popularity of midget racing declined in the post-war years. Thankfully, the United States Auto Club (USAC) stepped in in 1956, and helped to keep midget racing alive. The USAC is today one of the largest sanctioning bodies in midget racing. In the 1960s, however, as stock car racing grew in exposure and popularity, the visibility of midget racing declined even more. Despite its ups and downs, midget races have endured and continue to be held to this day – a time that, arguably, finds these open-wheeled vehicles more popular than ever.

Big Names, Small Cars

Midgets are the smallest of the cars in the six USAC divisions. The others (from smallest to largest) are super modified, sprint, dirt car, late-model stock and Indy car. Some drivers race in several of these categories.

Today, many midget car drivers are becoming well-known, as fans turn out in droves for races all over the country, and cable television broadcasts many events.

Over the years, some drivers have become very recognizable – even some who haven't gone on to other forms of auto racing. One such racer is Ron "Sleepy" Tripp. He is a two-time winner of the Belleville Nationals, one of the most prestigious races in midget racing, held at Belleville High Banks, a racetrack in Kansas. Jeff Gordon is also a past winner at Belleville – he won it in 1990.

Just To Name A Few

In addition to Gordon, drivers who have gone from some form of midget racing to NASCAR include Ken Schrader, Kenny Irwin, Terry Labonte, Bobby Labonte and Tony Stewart.

Another midget luminary is Parnelli Jones, who went on to win the Indianapolis 500. Others include seven-time USAC midget champion Mel Kenyon, Indy star Mario Andretti, three-time USAC midget champion Jason Leffler (a 2001 Winston Cup rookie), five-time USAC midget champion Rich Vogler and current sensation Kasey Kahne. Kahne is the defending National Midget Car Series champion, and in 2001 became the first back-to-back winner of the prestigious "Night Before The 500" race since Gordon did it in 1989 and 1990. Keep your eyes and ears peeled for this young man as he continues to climb racing's ladder of success.

Robert Laberge/Allsport

Winston Cup rookie Jason Leffler was a three-time USAC midget champion before he made the jump to Winston Cup.

Quarter Midgets

Quarter midgets are a division under midgets, and are, as their name suggests, one quarter of the size of a midget car. Quarter midget cars weigh about 260 to

300 pounds, as opposed to full-size midgets, which weigh close to 1,000 pounds. The race tracks are small, too – generally 1/20 mile. Jeff Gordon began his racing career in quarter midgets, as did many of today's Winston Cup and Indy Racing League stars. These race cars are often seen as a proving ground that can help ambitious young drivers "step up" into the big leagues of racing.

Quarter midget drivers range in age from 5-16, and the sport attracts almost as many girls as boys. Quarter midget racing is generally considered a family affair. A youngster is the driver, while typically, a parent is the crew chief and siblings and other relatives or friends help out in the pit. Other adults handle scheduling and transportation issues.

Although it may seem dangerous to have 5-year-olds racing around a track at 40 mph, serious injuries rarely occur in quarter midget racing. Drivers are protected by mandatory roll cages, and wear full helmets, five-point harnesses, gloves, jackets, neck braces and wrist restraints. Also, every quarter midget racer must complete a mandatory driving course before he or she is allowed to compete on the racetrack.

AP/WWP

Roll cages and other restraints keep drivers safe and secure.

The main association for quarter midget racing is the Quarter Midgets of America, which was incorporated in 1960 and today attracts more than 2,700 young drivers in the United States and Canada.

The Color Of Money

Why do so many drivers leave midgets to drive in other series? Well, for one thing, it's hard to make a living driving midgets. As opposed to the six-figure prizes that Winston Cup drivers often earn for winning a race, the typical purse for a midget race winner is $1,000 to $5,000. Considering that the cost of an average midget car ranges from $10,000 to $40,000 (not including the upkeep), it's easy to see the lure of NASCAR's big purses.

Unless they have a wealthy sponsor, it's very difficult for drivers to race midgets full time. Some of the best in the business have never been able to leave their day jobs.

The attention midget racing has been getting due to the success of drivers like Gordon and Tony Stewart, however, has helped to increase both the recognition and the purses for midget racing. Cable television has also helped the sport. According to one

Gordon went from racing on dirt tracks to winning $1 million at Las Vegas Motor Speedway.

car owner, "There's more and more midget racing on TV. I think that's given us a foothold. It's made people at the local tracks ask, 'Why aren't these cars here?'"

Fit For A King

When ESPN began broadcasting midget races in 1989, Richard Petty was reportedly a fan, saying, "We close down the shop every Thursday, stoke up the barbecue, and sit around and watch those crazy cats in their open-wheel cars. I wouldn't want to get in one, but I wouldn't miss watching 'em."

The Cars Of Today

On the surface, the midget cars of the 21st century aren't all that different from the cars that were raced back in the 1930s. They weigh about the same and have the same wheelbase, although the engines and chassis have changed with new technology. In terms of safety, though, the cars have improved tremendously as a result of improvements in technology and stricter sanctioning by officials. Thanks to these changes, the chances of a driver being seriously injured or killed have been reduced tremendously, although it still happens occasionally.

Are you interested in midget racing? Check for the races on your local sports networks or racetrack and find out what the excitement is all about!

Both boys and girls enjoy the sport of midget racing, including Sarah Fisher.

GET THE
GORDON GOODS

Sponsors And Endorsements

NASCAR is big business for the companies that sponsor Winston Cup drivers. Jeff Gordon not only has his car plastered with his sponsor's decals, he also wears their logos and pitches their products. Let's take a look at the world of sponsorship and endorsements.

Before the fire and flames, Gordon wore a rainbow wardrobe for primary sponsor DuPont.

AP/WWP

In Winston Cup racing, sponsors are a necessity. To be competitive on the circuit means having the best employees and the best equipment, and that takes money – a lot of money.

Primary Sponsors

Primary sponsors are the sponsors that are most prominently displayed on the driver's car and uniform. Gordon's primary sponsor is DuPont Automotive Finishes, and it has been since he entered Winston Cup racing in 1992.

Primary sponsors can pay over $10 million for the right to sponsor a particular team. Is it worth it? Well, their brand name reaches millions of people every time their driver gets into his or her

AP/WWP

Don't scratch the hood! DuPont pays millions of dollars to have the company's name and logo splashed across the front of Gordon's Monte Carlo.

race car, is interviewed or makes an appearance (Gordon wears his uniform at many of his appearances). That's pretty good publicity – and sponsors take advantage of it. According to an industry expert, "DuPont has made [NASCAR] an integral part of its marketing program. They're getting their customers at the races." And NASCAR fans are a loyal bunch. A recent survey showed that approximately 70% of NASCAR fans use NASCAR sponsor's products, so it's a good bet that sponsors get their money's worth.

Associate Sponsors

So what are all those other decals on Gordon's car? Those

The Downside Of Success

Some critics feel that the mega-bucks corporations spend on sponsorships force drivers to tone down or censor comments that could cause trouble in corporate America. One driver, who refused to be named, has said, "If you said what you really wanted to say, you'd probably lose your sponsor . . . It's like wearing a gag."

are his associate sponsors. They don't pay quite as much money as DuPont, so their decals are smaller. Gordon's associate sponsors include Pepsi-Cola, Fritos, Hendrick Motorsports, Delphi, Quaker State, SDRC, GMAC, Kelloggs, HAAS Automation, Inc., Chevrolet and The Hendrick Marrow Program.

In exchange for their sponsorship, Gordon has to fulfil many obligations to his sponsors – obligations that go beyond sporting their logos on his car. At the beginning of every season, drivers sign a contract with their sponsors listing how many appearances that driver is obligated to do for them. Drivers also appear in commercials and print ads for their sponsors, showing their support for the products and services their sponsors provide.

Associate sponsor Pepsi gets positive exposure when Gordon celebrates a win.

Not Camera Shy

Today, Gordon enjoys being on television, but that wasn't always the case. He has said, "When I was younger, I was the shyest kid on the block, so getting in front of a TV camera was the last thing I wanted to do."

The Joy Of Pepsi

Gordon's biggest associate sponsor is Pepsi, and he has done several endorsements and television commercials for the soft drink giant. He has appeared in a string of Pepsi commercials, including a spot aired during Super Bowl XXXIII in 1999. Gordon also appeared in an ad for Pepsi's "Joy of Cola" campaign with the ringleted young actress Hallie Kate Eisenberg. The spot, which debuted during the 1999 Pepsi 400, was entitled "Finish Line" and featured a thirsty Gordon who can't stop thinking about the refreshing Pepsi waiting for him at the finish line. Near the end of the race, however, Hallie shows up (on a bicycle!) and events take a surprising turn. According to a Pepsi marketing executive, "Jeff's vibrant personality and his rising popularity make him the perfect addition to the Joy of Cola campaign."

Also in 1999, Gordon drove a No. 24 Pepsi Chevrolet in five Busch Series races. In 2001, there's been even bigger exposure for Pepsi, this time in the Winston Cup Series. In 2000, Gordon and Hendrick Motorsports signed a five-year agreement, under which Gordon will race the No. 24 Pepsi car in two Winston Cup races per season. At the time, Gordon said of the deal, "I had a ton of fun racing the Pepsi car in the Busch Series and it's going to be exciting for all race fans to see

Making History

When Gordon drove the No. 24 Pepsi car in the Talladega 500, it marked the first time a Pepsi car had appeared in the Winston Cup Series since 1983, when Darrell Waltrip drove the Pepsi Challenger car.

a Pepsi car race a couple of times in the Winston Cup next year. If it's anything like my latest Pepsi commercial, my only worry is that Hallie and her grandpa might catch me on their bike."

After sponsoring Gordon on the Busch circuit, Pepsi returned to Winston Cup in 2001.

Gordon drove the Winston Cup Pepsi car for the first time in the Talladega 500 on April 22, 2001. In a statement, Gordon said, "We had two great years in the Busch Series, and I'm thrilled to take Pepsi back to the Winston Cup Series. With a little luck, we can bring the No. 24 Pepsi car back to Victory Lane." It was not to be on that day, but there's little doubt that fans will soon be seeing the unique car in a Victory Lane celebration.

The car sported a "Pepsi Blue" paint scheme with a special Pearlescent Blue color developed by Dupont. The Pepsi car's next scheduled appearance was in the Pepsi 400 at Daytona International Speedway on July 7.

The Face On The Cereal Box

Gordon's winning smile has made him a natural spokesman for toothpaste products.

AP/WWP

If you didn't catch any of Gordon's Pepsi ads, don't worry. There are plenty of other places where you can see his famous face. For example, Gordon has appeared on the front of boxes of Kellogg's Frosted Mini Wheats cereal and on several boxes of Close-Up toothpaste (showing off his white teeth, of course).

Why would a toothpaste company choose someone like Gordon to endorse their product? Well, according to Close-Up's brand manager, they wanted Gordon because of "his social confidence and youthful appeal. Plus, he has white teeth. I won't name any names, but we didn't want somebody older who had been chewing tobacco all of his life."

The Flavor King

No plain vanilla ice cream for Jeff Gordon! According to Edy's Grand Ice Cream, his favorite ingredients are marshmallows, almonds, fudge swirls, caramel swirls, walnuts, strawberries, bananas and chocolate shavings!

Apparently, eating ice cream all of his life is a different story, because there's even a flavor of ice cream named for Gordon! In 1999, Edy's (also known as Dreyer's) Ice Cream ran a contest in which fans of the No. 24 Dupont and its driver could send in their own ideas for a flavor and name. Gordon chose the winner – Jeff's Mint Chocolate Speedway – from five

finalists in April of 2000. He said, "I'm thrilled to have such a unique relationship with Dreyer's and Edy's . . . it's fun having an ice cream flavor named after you." Edy's had previously put Gordon's picture on their cartons and named several flavors for him, including "Jeff's Rocky Road," "Sweet Victory Sundae" and "Checkered Flag Sundae."

Fritos, one of Gordon's associate sponsors, took advantage of their relationship in the summer of 1999 when Fritos created a product called "Fritos Racerz" – race car–shaped Fritos chips with the No. 24 imprinted on them. Who was seen on television promoting the new product? None other than Jeff Gordon, of course!

Another associate sponsor of the No. 24 car recently stepped into the spotlight. The new Chicagoland Speedway announced in March, 2001 that it had signed a four-year sponsorship agreement with Tropicana products and that its inaugural NASCAR Winston Cup race would be the Tropicana 400. Gordon, who is a spokesman for Tropicana Season's Best juice (which is the official juice of Jeff Gordon and the No. 24 racing team), was on hand in Chicago when the announcement was made and played an interesting role – he answered phones and took race ticket

Safety First

For several years, Gordon, an avid boater, has teamed up with Bombardier Recreational Product's National Safe Boating Campaign, filming television public service announcements for the Sea-Doo "Boat Smart From The Start" program. In 2000, he received a special award from Bombardier in recognition of his contributions to boating safety efforts.

orders from surprised fans! He also unveiled the official Tropicana 400 race logo and welcomed Tropicana's sponsorship.

In The Winner's Circle

Gordon also does endorsements for some NASCAR collectibles. In 1999, he signed a five-year agreement with Hasbro Inc., which markets the Winner's Circle brand of racing memorabilia. With the agreement, Gordon, who is the most recognized NASCAR driver among boys aged 6 to 11, will appear in ads for Winner's Circle toy cars, playsets, puzzles and electronic games.

Who's That Behind Those FosterGrants?

One of Gordon's latest endorsement deals is with sunglasses giant FosterGrant. In April of 2001, Gordon signed a multi-year endorsement and licensing deal with the company. Look for him in a "Who's That Behind Those FosterGrants?" ad in the spring of 2002. In addition to the advertisements, FosterGrant will also create a line of sunglasses to be endorsed by Gordon, as well as a sunglasses collection featuring the No. 24 and the Dupont No. 24 car colors.

Even behind dark sunglasses, Jeff Gordon's winning attitude is unmistakable.

"An Advertiser's Dream"

So what is it about Jeff Gordon that makes him so appealing to sponsors and manufacturers? According to Fred Wagenhals, CEO of Action Performance, Inc., it's his clean-cut image. Said Wagenhals, "Gordon is a young kid, has a wonderful family and women are probably buying 50 percent

What's Good For The Goose . . .

Gordon's endorsements and visibility are not only good for him, but for the sport of stock car racing as well. For instance, every time Pepsi uses him in a national commercial, NASCAR receives free publicity that otherwise would have cost it millions of dollars!

of his product. That's what NASCAR has going for it. Right now it's a sport where its drivers are clean-cut. You don't read about them in the paper with drug problems, beating their wives." That's not all. A 1998 article in a marketing trade magazine stated that, "Beyond being a winning driver, Gordon is blessed with the charm and charisma that transforms an athlete from star athlete to celebrity."

AP/WWP

Gordon's youth, ability and looks make
him a top choice with manufacturers and sponsors.

And Bob Williams, president of Burns Sports, a firm that unites advertisers and athletes in promotional deals, has said of Gordon, "He really is the first driver who has demonstrated the staying power to cross over from the world of NASCAR to compete against the very elite athletes . . . Because of his looks, he has a strong appeal to men and women, much like Jim Palmer did in the underwear ads. Simply put, he's an advertiser's dream."

And Gordon knows it. "I know I have a hand in NASCAR's success. I simply try to put on as good of a race as I possibly can, but I do it for the fans. If it weren't for my fans supporting me, spending money, going to my races, Jeff Gordon wouldn't be anybody," said Gordon. "Those people are special. They keep me hungry and working hard. And we're glad for it!

Gordon has emerged as one of NASCAR's most popular spokesmen.

ImageDirect

Cars Through The Years

Jeff Gordon is arguably best-known for the rainbow paint scheme, DuPont-sponsored Chevrolet that he drove between 1993 and 2000. But Gordon has driven cars sponsored by other companies, and has even driven cars by manufacturers other than Chevrolet! Here's a look at some of the many cars Jeff Gordon has raced during his successful career.

Gordon drove this Pontiac Grand Prix in the Busch Series in 1990.

He raced the Carolina Ford Dealers Ford Thunderbird in the Busch Series in 1991.

Baby Ruth candy bars sponsored Gordon's Ford Thunderbird in the 1992 Busch Series.

Bill Hall/Allsport

In 1993, Jeff Gordon drove a Chevy Lumina on his way to
Rookie of the Year Winston Cup honors.

J.D. Cuban/Allsport

Gordon had years and years of success behind the wheel
of his rainbow-colored Chevrolet Monte Carlo.

AP/WWP

The special Chroma Premier car was a
winner at the 1997 Busch Clash.

Gordon raced this car, with a
paint scheme promoting the
1997 movie "Jurassic Park," to
victory at the Coca-Cola 600.

Craig Jones/Allsport

The 50th anniversary of NASCAR was commemorated on the hood of
Gordon's DuPont ChromaLusion Chevrolet Monte Carlo in 1998.

David Taylor/Allsport

Gordon drove a Pepsi-sponsored Monte Carlo
in his 1999 return to the Busch Series.

AP/WWP

The Force was with Gordon and his
1999 Star Wars Episode 1 Busch car.

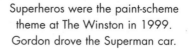

Superheros were the paint-scheme
theme at The Winston in 1999.
Gordon drove the Superman car.

The NASCAR Racers cartoon was featured on Gordon's car at the 1999 Pennzoil 400.

The new millennium was celebrated with a special silver paint scheme in 2000.

This twist on the DuPont rainbow paint scheme was raced at the
Coca-Cola 600 at Lowe's Motor Speedway on May 28, 2000.

Robert Laberge/Allsport

The 50th anniversary of the "Peanuts" comic strip was honored with a special paint job on August 5, 2000, at the Brickyard 400 at Indianapolis Motor Speedway.

Robert Laberge/Allsport

Goodbye, rainbow – hello, fire and flames! Gordon's new
DuPont paint scheme was unveiled for the 2001 Winston Cup season.

Bugs Bunny and Elmer Fudd
accompanied Gordon at the
Chevrolet Monte Carlo 400 in 2001.

Gordon Memorabilia

Jeff Gordon is indisputably one of the most popular NASCAR drivers around, and his face and racing gear are easily recognizable. It's no wonder that you can find his likeness or logo on products ranging from action figures and die-cast cars to plush toys and apparel, sporting goods and Christmas tree ornaments!

A Racetrack In Your Living Room

Zoom zoom! You can pretend you're Jeff Gordon passing Dale Earnhardt Jr. on those high-banked turns at Bristol Motor Speedway as you maneuver your replica DuPont Monte Carlo on an imaginary track in your living room. Die-cast models of all of Gordon's cars are available in sizes ranging from 1:24 scale to 1:64 scale (the same size as those cars you played with in your youth) and even as small as 1:144! If

it's Gordon's new fire-and-flames paint scheme or his classic rainbow look, the famous "Jurassic Park" car that he raced to victory at The Winston in 1997 or a sprint car from his early days, you can find them produced by such manufacturers as Action, Revell or Winner's Circle.

Cars are not the only die-cast Gordon products on the market. Gas pumps, Chevy Suburbans, Chevy Tahoes, haulers, duallies and trailers, all sporting Gordon's many familiar paint schemes, are available for purchase. Many of these items (and the cars, too) serve double duty as banks, as well.

You can't race a car without a driver, and with the help of manufacturers like Kenner, Jeff Gordon action figures are easy to come by. One of the most valuable action figures is a 12-inch Kenner special edition that is valued in the $100 price range! Most action figures, however, can be found for around $20 in department stores and hobby shops.

Of course, your imaginary track wouldn't be complete without the pit crew! Winner's Circle has several sets of figurines of Gordon's crew.

Apparel

What better way to show your support for Gordon than to wear it with pride? T-shirts and baseball caps are abundantly available on-line, at stores and, of course, trackside. They come in a rainbow of colors and usually range in price from about $10 to $25. Along with basic styles featuring Gordon's name, photo and car, manufacturers have also developed more specific designs. Wear them with pride!

Good For Home Or Office

Turn your computer area into a racetrack with a Jeff Gordon mouse and mouse pad. The big and bold "24" on the mouse pad will let all your curious co-workers know who your favorite driver is, while the mouse is shaped like Gordon's Monte Carlo. A set consisting of a mouse, mouse pad and screen saver costs just under $50.

Americraft Pewter Accessories and Montana Silversmiths produce a variety of Jeff Gordon belt buckles, all of which are officially licensed by NASCAR. Americraft buckles feature a Gordon theme on the front and a short write-up about him on the back. They currently offer more than 40 different buckles. The Montana collection offers buckles in many different shapes and sizes to accentuate formal or casual attire. Most buckles sell in the $15 to $20 range and are available through trackside vendors or hobby shops that sell NASCAR merchandise.

Something For Every Room In Your Home

Time flies when Jeff Gordon races, but you can keep track of it with a Gordon clock! JEBCO, the premier manufacturer of NASCAR-licensed clocks, has an extensive collection of Gordon merchandise. In addition to mounted clocks, die-cast replicas of Gordon's famous No. 24 car also come in the form of an AM/FM clock radio!

When you're watching Gordon take the checkered flag at Sears Point Raceway, you need something to put that ice-cold Pepsi in. How about a Gordon beverage container? The number of different cups and mugs featuring Gordon's name and logo are seemingly endless – shot glasses, coffee cups, ceramic steins, insulated plastic or stainless steel travel mugs – the list goes on and on! Within these subdivisions there are many varieties of color, size and design. The prices are as varied as

Gordon Hits A Home Run!

Jeff Gordon probably isn't much of a baseball player (where would he find the time?), but if he was, he'd probably use an officially licensed baseball made by ProBall, Inc. It comes in a clear plastic cover mounted on a stand designed to look like a car tire. The Gordon ball is imprinted with No. 24 as well as a replica of Gordon's signature.

the designs. A basic plastic cup by Motorsport Direct Racing Collectibles sells for around $5, whereas a more sleek stainless steel mug by Racing USA costs about $25.

Posters are one of the most popular Jeff Gordon products available. Posters are colorful, inexpensive and look great wherever you hang them. With just a little searching and a lot of wall space you can find posters of Gordon, his car or his crew to decorate your room. Even the largest posters are still affordable. A giant six-foot tall door poster will only cost you about $15. There are also motivational posters for sale that emphasize teamwork that will inspire any Gordon fan.

There's even a Gordon Christmas ornament from Hallmark for you to hang on your tree! Featuring Gordon and his car, the ornament is poised to capture the checkered flag. This ornament, released in 1997, was the first in a series that included fellow racing legends Richard Petty and Bill Elliott. Like most ornaments, it was only available for one year, so you won't be able to find it on the shelves of your local retail stores. But with the right combination of luck and patience, this ornament can be hanging in your collection soon!

Satisfy Your Sweet Tooth

Whether you know the company as Edy's or Dreyer's, you'll recognize the container because it has Gordon's car on the front! They've come up with several racing-themed flavors, including "Sweet Victory Sundae" and "Checkered Flag Sundae." The latest flavor to be found in cones everywhere is "Jeff's Mint Chocolate Speedway," which won a taste test for which Gordon was a judge.

Sporting Gear

Speaking of his reverence for the late Dale Earnhardt, Gordon said, "As little as I enjoy fishing, I still enjoyed listening to him talk about fishing." Do you think they talked about Jeff Gordon fishing lures? Functional lures manufactured by Oxboro Outdoors and fully licensed by NASCAR are vibrant and colorful. One features Gordon's photo and signature, while another is decorated with a picture of his car. Collectors can also find a novelty fishing lure in the size of a 1:144 die cast of the No. 24 Monte Carlo. This lure isn't intended to catch you any fish, however – just envious looks from other Gordon collectors. Lures usually cost less than $8.

If there's one thing an angler needs while out on the pond, it's a pocket knife, and a Jeff Gordon pocket knife is perfect. Many knives, including ones with handles in the shape of Gordon's car, can be purchased for as little as $20. Knives are made by several well-known manufacturers, including Action and Case Racing Collectibles.

Toys For Kids Of All Ages

We all know that one of Gordon's favorite activities away from the racetrack is playing video games. Do you think he plays "Jeff Gordon's XS Racin," by ASC Games? In this game, you compete against worthy rivals on a racetrack located in the future, while getting valuable tactical information from Gordon himself. Once you've blown away your competition, you can match wits against your master, Gordon. Who will emerge the victor?

Or maybe Gordon prepares for race day by practicing with a No. 24 radio-controlled car.

It's Jeff Gordon Time!

A watch is the perfect purchase for a Gordon fan. Many different styles are available to choose from – wrist or pocket, leather or metal band, in many different colors and sizes. Find them by manufacturers such as Sportivi, Montana Silversmiths and Sun Time, among others at the track, racing collector stores, on-line or through catalogs.

Battery-powered, this car can go anywhere you can find a track! Speed forward, turn in reverse. The car is made of heavy-duty construction in case you "hit the wall." You can find radio-controlled cars by toy maker Hasbro at any toy store.

If something a little more low-key is what you prefer in your toys, how about a puzzle or plush doll? The first Gordon puzzles were manufactured by Milton Bradley. Today, you can find several jigsaw puzzles produced by Winner's Circle (who are also known for their die-cast cars). Beginner puzzle fans can test their skills on a simple 200-piece puzzle, while more experienced puzzlers can challenge themselves with the Puzz3D series by Winner's Circle. These puzzles let you put together a three-dimensional reproduction of Gordon's race car and are perfect for passing the time on a rainy afternoon.

Plush figures are both collectible and huggable and are growing in popularity by leaps and bounds. Gordon fans can find No. 24–themed plush bears dressed in T-shirts or driver suits in a number of sizes, shapes and colors. Plush figures also come in the shape of Gordon's car and even Gordon himself! Well-known manufacturers such as Racing Champions, Action Performance and Team Up International, among others, have begun putting these collectibles on the market. They're available at hobby shops, Internet sites and tracks around the country.

No matter what your preference to show the world that Jeff Gordon is your favorite NASCAR driver, you can show that you root for him in a number of ways!

Fans Of The No. 24

NASCAR fans are some of the most loyal and passionate in the sports world, and fans of Jeff Gordon and his No. 24 DuPont ride are no different. Let's step inside the fans' world and find out just why they love Jeff Gordon.

They Love To Watch

For Tanya Harmon, of Smyrna, Tennessee, 1999 was the year she saw the light. She had just begun to get interested in NASCAR, and noticed that one man's name kept coming up over and over again. That name was Jeff Gordon. Tanya decided that she'd better keep her eye on this young driver, who'd won the Winston Cup championship the previous year. She says, "I watched even more races in 2000 and quickly found out that a person was either for Jeff Gordon or was against him, and I was for him." The reason? "There was something about Jeff that caught my attention," she says. "His

Tanya Harmon is a serious Jeff Gordon fan.

Jeff Gordon On Being Himself

"If I was phony, then I would be out here in my Wranglers saying how much I love fishing and deer hunting. I'm just trying to be myself . . . If you like what I stand for and the things that I do, then support me. If you don't, I understand. I know I'm not going to get every fan out there in the stands to follow me."

character, thankfulness to God and how he freely showed his emotions gave witness that Jeff is also a wonderful person in addition to a great race car driver." These days, Tanya has caught Jeff Gordon fever and is firmly entrenched in her fandom. She says, "My car is adorned with a No. 24 flag and I try not to mimic Jeff's racing moves while driving through town."

Another Gordon fan, Gail Benjamin of Dallas, has been watching him tear up the racetracks since 1992. She says, "I wish I could say that I have followed Jeff Gordon since he raced the midget cars. Unfortunately, I didn't learn of him until he came to NASCAR racing in 1992. I became a fan in 1994 because of his amazing driving abilities and his fast crew. To be straight up, he's a hell of a driver! He just won't stop! Usually, drivers come in with a bang and then go silent. Not Jeff! He just keeps on winning!"

Gail Benjamin has been a fan of Gordon's since he made his NASCAR debut!

A Shrine To No. 24

Some fans express their loyalty to Gordon by decorating their homes with Gordon paraphernalia of all sorts. One couple, profiled in the *Charlotte Observer*, has done just that. According to the article, Diane and Walter Witt

AP/WWP

Renowned artist Sam Bass designed the paint schemes for Gordon's rainbow car and the fire-and-flames car. Here he puts his signature on a Gordon print in 2000.

of Tennessee have hung a sign on their porch proclaiming it "Jeff Gordon Boulevard." The porch is also home to life-size cutouts of Gordon, as well as a 9-by-7–foot oil painting of him and his No. 24 Chevrolet Monte Carlo. The final touch of their collection rests in the yard beside the porch. There sits an autographed Chevy Cavalier painted in the colors of Gordon's car, housed in a glass case adorned with flags and red, blue, green and orange lights.

Inside the house are dozens of framed photos and cutouts of Gordon, miniature DuPont cars hanging from the ceiling and a curio cabinet filled with Gordon plates, bowls, mugs and glasses.

Mrs. Witt admits, "People say I'm crazy all the time. I have a lot of fun with it." The Witts say that some people have mistaken their home for a memorabilia store and just walked in the front door. The Witts don't mind.

Mrs. Witt became a fan in 1993, when her brother-in-law was recuperating from surgery and watched the races at her house. He told her to pick a car to follow and she chose the No. 24 DuPont because of all the colors. At the time, her brother-in-law laughed at her, saying Gordon was just a rookie. Bet he's not laughing now! And what keeps Mrs. Witt coming back to Gordon year after year? "Whether he wins or not, he'll thank the Lord for a good race. You want somebody to be a good role model."

Another fan's obsession began after she met Jeff Gordon at SeaWorld. The fan, Cathy King-Chupakoff of St. Cloud, Florida, was profiled in a March 2001 *Orlando Sentinel* article. She convinced her husband to create a NASCAR room in their home, where she has, among other items, a *NASCAR Illustrated* magazine cover signed by Gordon after he won the Daytona 500 in 1997. Her prized possession is an Apple Jacks cereal box with Gordon on the front. Why is it special? Because King-Chupakoff (who saw the box first) had to argue with a man in a grocery store who also wanted it.

Why They Love Him

What makes Gordon's fans stay with him through the ups and downs (mostly ups) and all the harassment they get from from fans of other NASCAR drivers? According to one fan, "He's just a good, hard, smooth driver." That, coupled with Gordon's charm and graciousness to his fans, makes him a tough act to beat!

Some fans, like Craig Maraldo from Las Vegas, devote entire rooms of their homes to their Gordon memorabilia collections!

The Jeff Gordon Fan Club

Do you want to get even more enjoyment out of being a Jeff Gordon fan? Then become a member of the official Jeff Gordon Fan Club – "the hottest fan club today."

The official Jeff Gordon Fan Club (JGFC) is easy to join and fun to be a part of! Those who sign up for the JGFC will receive a membership kit full of goodies. The kit includes a welcome letter, membership card, quarterly JGFC newsletter, a dated JGFC lapel pin and JGFC patch, Post-it Notes, a cap and a Koozie. In addition to all that, you also get club money, which you can put toward purchases you make at the racetrack when you make the journey to root for Gordon in person!

Jeff Gordon celebrates his victory at the UAW Daimler Chrysler 400 at Las Vegas Motor Speedway in 2001.

Membership runs from January 1 to December 31, and includes lots of fun fan events throughout the year. 2001's events included an opportunity to meet with Gordon and hear him speak about his hopes for the year before the season-opening Daytona 500, as well as a question-and-answer session with Gordon for 130 fan club members before the UAW-Daimler Chrysler 400 at Las Vegas Motor Speedway. Door prizes were given out and an autograph session was held for the excited fans in attendance.

It's easy to root for someone as fan-friendly as Jeff Gordon!

Don't miss out on any more of the action! Sign up for the Jeff Gordon Fan Club today! Send a check or money order for $25.49 (made payable to Action Sports Image, LLC) to:

Jeff Gordon Fan Club

6301 Performance Drive
Concord, North Carolina 28027

1-877-JEFF-GORDON

Photo Index

Use this index to find photographs of individuals and racetracks depicted in this book. Pages are listed in numerical order.

Photo Index